P9-CMD-678

Bigelow's
Build Your Own PC
Pocket Reference

Other Titles in Stephen J. Bigelow's Pocket Reference Series

Bigelow's
Build Your Own PC
Pocket Reference

Stephen J. Bigelow

McGraw-Hill

New York   San Francisco   Washington, D.C.   Auckland   Bogotá
Caracas   Lisbon   London   Madrid   Mexico City   Milan
Montreal   New Delhi   San Juan   Singapore
Sydney   Tokyo   Toronto

Library of Congress Cataloging-in-Publication Data

Bigelow, Stephen J.
    Bigelow's build your own PC pocket reference / Stephen J. Bigelow.
        p.   cm.
    Includes index.
    ISBN 0-07-037139-3
    1. Microcomputers—Design and construction—Amateurs' manuals.
    2. IBM-compatible computers—Design and construction—Amateurs'
    manuals.   I. Title.
    TK9969.B54   1998
    621.39'16—dc21   97-48321
                                                                   CIP

McGraw-Hill

*A Division of The **McGraw·Hill** Companies*

    4 5 6 7 8 9 0   DOC/DOC   9 0 3 2 1 0 9 8

ISBN 0-07-037139-3

The sponsoring editor for this book was Scott L. Grillo, the editing supervisor was Penny Linskey, and the production supervisor was Tina Cameron. It was set in New Century Schoolbook by Don Feldman of McGraw-Hill's Professional Book Group composition unit.

Printed and bound by R. R. Donnelley & Sons Company.

Disclaimer and Cautions

It is IMPORTANT that you read and understand the following information. Please read it carefully!

PERSONAL RISK AND LIMITS OF LIABILITY
The repair of personal computers and their peripherals involves some amount of personal risk. Use **extreme** caution when working with ac and high-voltage power sources. Every reasonable effort has been made to identify and reduce areas of personal risk. You are instructed to read this book carefully before attempting the procedures discussed. If you are uncomfortable following the procedures that are outlined in this book, **do not attempt them**—refer your service to qualified service personnel.

NEITHER THE AUTHOR, THE PUBLISHER, NOR ANYONE DIRECTLY OR INDIRECTLY CONNECTED WITH THE PUBLICATION OF THIS BOOK SHALL MAKE ANY WARRANTY EITHER EXPRESSED OR IMPLIED, WITH REGARD TO THIS MATERIAL INCLUDING, BUT NOT LIMITED TO, THE IMPLIED WARRANTIES OF QUALITY, MERCHANTABILITY, AND FITNESS FOR ANY PARTICULAR PURPOSE. Further, neither the author, publisher, nor anyone directly or indirectly connected with the publication of this book shall be liable for errors or omissions contained herein, or for incidental or consequential damages, injuries, or financial or material losses resulting from the use, or inability to use, the material contained herein. This material is provided AS IS, and the reader bears all responsibilities and risks connected with its use.

Contents

Preface

There is no doubt that personal computers are now a fact of life—whether at work, at home, or at play, the PC has a place. Sooner or later, you're going to need a new computer or replace an aging model that can no longer be upgraded. In many cases, PCs are purchased outright from major retailers or wholesalers for very reasonable prices, but before you pick up that telephone and warm up your credit card, there are some very compelling reasons to *build* your next PC for close to what it would cost you to buy it outright.

- *You can do it yourself.* The spirit of the do it yourselfer is certainly not dead when it comes to computer building. Building your own PC from the ground up makes you the master of your own destiny, allowing you to proceed at your own pace and use the components of your choice. Unlike automobiles, you don't need any special tools, and you don't even get your hands dirty.

- *You know what you're getting.* I hate to say it, but PC salespeople are often woefully uninformed about the systems they're selling. I've seen so many occasions where new PC buyers have been "burned" by well-meaning but technically limited sales information and support. Building your own PC allows you to select each and every part that goes into the system.

■ *You get an invaluable learning experience.*   If you've ever looked at computer courses at local schools and colleges, you already know how expensive education can be. Building your own PC gives you a hands on introduction to the inner workings of a contemporary PC and you even get to keep the PC.

■ *You prepare yourself for upgrades and troubleshooting.*   I don't know about you, but I hate being at the mercy of other people. If you've ever been frustrated by slow, expensive repair shops, you can appreciate the savings in upgrading or repairing your own PC. Building the PC yourself typically makes you more familiar with the inside of the PC than some $40 to $60/hour bench technician.

■ *You can customize your PC.*   PC builders typically offer a limited number of PC "packages." It is possible to select alternate components, but that usually carries a premium that can boost the cost of your new system by hundreds of dollars (and delay the system by weeks). Building your own PC lets you select a specific combination of components and features that suits *your* specific needs.

■ *You can be starting on a money-making hobby.* Custom-built PCs are very popular, and if you find that you've got the aptitude for PC building, there's always an opportunity for you to take on commercial PC building as a sideline or pastime.

No matter what motivates you to build your own PC, this book is designed to be a convenient, step-by-step guide and reference that will help you tackle almost any conventional PC construction. Using the steps outlined in this book, you will be able to understand the important issues involved in component selection and choose components with confidence, to build up the system hardware using a thoughtful, proven procedure that will minimize any potential errors and to then install and optimize an operating system. This book also contains solutions to the most common assembly problems. I am interested in *your* success, so you can find me at

Dynamic Learning Systems
P.O. Box 282
Jefferson, MA 01522-0282
Internet:sbigelow@cerfnet.com

Or visit the *Dynamic Learning Systems* web site at http://www.dlspubs.com

Stephen J. Bigelow

1

Choosing
the Parts

The most vital part of any new construction or upgrade project is the "planning" phase. You can choose *any* parts for your new computer, but choosing the *right* parts to fit *your* particular needs can sometimes be a real headache. This first part of the book outlines the many diverse subassemblies involved in a typical PC and is designed to help you select the devices that will satisfy your needs.

So You Want to Build Your Own PC

Should I buy it, or should I build it myself? That's a question I hear all too often—and it's probably the best way to start this chapter. The PC industry is cutthroat and relentlessly competitive, so prices for premanufactured PCs are very low. As a result, a home-built PC is rarely cheaper than a comparable store-bought model. Therefore, before you rush out and start buying components, you should consider the advantages and disadvantages.

Disadvantages

PC building is not for the faint of heart. Home-built PCs often can cost several hundred dollars more than a store-bought system. This is because PC makers buy parts in quantities of tens of thousands—you just can't touch their volume discounts. Next, PC building requires patience and a commitment of time and effort. If you need a PC *now* for some specific purpose, building it yourself may not be the right choice.

Advantages

On the other hand, building your own system offers some compelling advantages. The biggest advantages are practical *education* and personal *satisfaction*—there's nothing quite like watching your own PC come together from the ground up and knowing that you've done the work yourself. You also get the chance to learn your PC inside and out. This can pay dividends later when the PC needs to be upgraded or repaired. Because you already know your system, you are uniquely qualified to perform the upgrade or tackle the repair (which can be a huge cost savings over having someone else do it). Another advantage is *customization*—that is, you can tailor your system for your own unique needs and avoid the prepackaged deals that PC vendors offer.

The bottom line

Ultimately, you'll spend a little more to build your own PC, but the educational value and personal satisfaction you'll receive are often well worth it. If you still need help making your decision whether or not to build, answer the builder's checklist below:

- Do you enjoy a new learning challenge?
- Do you want to understand how a PC is assembled?

- Do you want a PC to have particular features but can't find those features in prepackaged systems?

- Do you enjoy working your way through some possible problems such as those that might occur during a new PC construction?

- Do you want to interact with a variety of vendors and distributors?

- Have you ever thought of custom PC building as a sideline or small business?

- Is education worth spending a few extra dollars for?

- Are you comfortable working with wiring and mechanical assemblies?

If you answered Yes to six or more questions, you're probably ready to build your own PC.

Deciding to Upgrade

Although the economics of building your own PC from scratch may not always be appealing, the economics of *upgrading* are often much clearer—especially for systems that are only a few years old. Once again, there are some advantages and disadvantages to consider before you walk into a store.

Disadvantages

The most apparent issue with upgrades is compatibility—with PC technology advancing so fast (PCs tend to double their capacity every 18 to 24 months), it is sometimes difficult to upgrade an older PC with current parts. If you've ever struggled with configuring an EIDE hard drive in an older Integrated Drive Electronics (IDE) system or tried to find more memory for your proprietary PC, you already get the picture. Forget about finding older parts for your upgrade— only the latest and greatest are available off the shelf.

You might get lucky visiting a PC auction, swap meet, or yard sale, but that's about it.

Advantages

There are strong economic reasons to upgrade a PC—it's *cheaper* to upgrade than it is to buy or build a *new* system. By upgrading, you can improve the capabilities and performance of your current PC (sometimes dramatically). In many cases, a good upgrade may allow you to get another 6 to 12 months or more from your current system. If you plan your upgrade strategy carefully, you may even be able to use the upgrade parts in a new system later on. Upgrading also requires less time than building, and the potential for problems is generally smaller than with new constructions.

Upgrading by troubleshooting

The trouble with such fast technological progress is that parts rarely stay on the shelf long. That video board you bought last year is no longer available. How about that 4X CD-ROM drive you put in some time back? Today there's something newer and faster in its place. When your PC fails and you need to replace a broken device, chances are that you'll *need* to upgrade simply because you cannot obtain an identical replacement device. From this standpoint, *upgrading* is often a proxy of troubleshooting.

Remember to recycle

Of course, there will come a point when spending the money on upgrades will not result in a worthwhile system improvement. Economists and engineers usually call this the point of diminishing returns, but my car mechanic just says, "you're not getting any bang for your buck." Either way, your obsolete system still has some life left in it. You can strip it down for parts for your new (or custom-built) PC. Or there is always a relative, child, school system, church group, amateur radio club, or any number of other places where your old PC would be *more* than welcome. The idea here is to never discard anything that is PC-related— somebody somewhere will want it.

The Issues with Troubleshooting

PC troubleshooting is perhaps the most complex, difficult, and *rewarding* part of working with PCs, but it is certainly not a pursuit for the meek. Still, with some understanding of how PCs work, what all the parts are, and how those parts go together (sort of like what you learn with this book), it *is* possible to master almost any PC problem.

Disadvantages

The main disadvantage to troubleshooting is that it requires patience and logic—there's no instant gratification here. To troubleshoot a PC (or anything else) successfully, you must be able to (1) understand the problem and (2) isolate the fault. Once you can identify where the problem is (or at least know where the problem is *not*), you can correct or replace the defective device quickly and efficiently. If you're unable to identify and isolate, I promise you that your troubleshooting experience will be an exercise in frustration. Fortunately, there are some terrific troubleshooting books to keep you pointed in the right direction.

Advantages

Sure, I could melt your heart telling you what a sense of personal accomplishment comes with troubleshooting, but if you're still not impressed, try this on for size—PC technicians get $40 to $60 per hour. Not only do you save a bundle of money by troubleshooting yourself, but you *know* what was done and whether the problem is fixed or not.

The golden rule of troubleshooting

Pssssst, come over here—I'm going to share a secret with you. There's *one* rule of troubleshooting that can save your behind more than any fancy test equipment or diagnostics. Ready? Here it is:

Change only *one* thing at a time

Remember when I said you need to isolate a problem in order to solve it? By changing only one thing at a time and then retesting the system, you can easily isolate the point at which a problem occurs (or is solved). For example, suppose you have a problem reading a floppy drive. If you swap the drive, cable, controller, and power supply all at the same time, you *may* fix the problem, but you'll never really know just *what* went wrong. But if you clean the drive first, then swap the cable, *then* replace the drive (testing each time you make a change), and so on, you might just find that cleaning would have been enough. The golden rule also holds true for upgrading.

The Contemporary PC

OK, you've made the decision to build your own PC. Before you make out that shopping list, let's cover the essential parts of the PC and talk about the role each component plays in the system. By the way, there's no such thing as an *unimportant* part. Everything serves a vital purpose and can have an impact on the overall performance and reliability of your system. You'll also find some notes on upgrade and troubleshooting considerations.

Case

Don't you dare laugh. It's certainly not the most glamorous part of the PC, but the case provides several important attributes. It offers structural integrity for *all* the elements in the system. Its air inlets and outlets largely define the air flow pattern that keep your system cool. The case supplies "hard" mounting points for drives. And—for many builders—the case defines the cosmetic "look" of the system.

Generally speaking, cases are not upgraded. They certainly *could* be, but you don't often see people turn to their spouse and say, "Honey, I'd really love a new case for my NEC 386SX." I mean, there's just so many other goodies that you can spend your money on. The time case upgrading becomes viable is if you're upgrading your motherboard, and you need a case that will accommodate the new motherboard. Another time you might like to upgrade your case is if you're doing a lot of physical expansion (i.e., adding a lot of drives to a system and need to replace a desktop with a minitower or full tower).

Power supply

Here's another component that goes largely ignored until it's too late. A power supply provides *all* of the energy needed by the computer, so there must be ample power to serve *everything* in the system; otherwise, the system may not work properly (if at all). You're pretty safe with a 250-watt (250-W) to 300-W power supply. There is more about choosing a power supply later in this chapter.

From a practical standpoint, power supply upgrades are a lot more common (and important) than you might think. Normally, a new power supply will have absolutely *no* impact on system performance (there's either enough energy to run the PC or there isn't). But if you plan to add a lot of new devices to the system, you may need a bigger power supply to handle the additional power demands. You may also need to match a new power supply and motherboard if the new motherboard requires advanced "power conservation" signals from the power supply.

Power supply problems can have a profound impact on your computer. An overloaded or failing power supply may cause erratic operation or may prevent the PC from starting entirely. The typical means of checking a power supply is to measure each of its outputs using a voltmeter. These measurements are taken while the PC is running and the power supply is connected to the motherboard. If any of the power supply outputs are low or absent, it usually means the power supply has failed and should be replaced. We'll have more troubleshooting pointers later in the book.

Motherboard

This is the heart of your system—the motherboard holds all of the key processing elements such as the Central Processing Unit (CPU), memory, cache, expansion busses, chipset, and so on. The motherboard almost entirely defines the performance of your system. You'll find that a motherboard is the single most expensive and important element of the PC, so choosing the "right" motherboard is a very important step in your construction project.

Because the majority of processing components are located on the motherboard, replacing the motherboard will yield the *greatest* performance improvement for your money. Motherboards also drop in price very quickly, so unless you need to buy the *very* latest motherboards, you can usually obtain a recent model relatively inexpensively. This makes motherboard upgrades surprisingly economical. Motherboard upgrades can usually be broken down into two levels: motherboard add-ons and motherboard replacement. Motherboard add-ons involve changing the things that are attached to your motherboard such as the CPU or your memory Single Inline Memory Modules (SIMMs) or adding cache. All of these things can improve the operation of your system using your current motherboard. Motherboard replacement (as the name implies) involves replacing the physical circuit board.

Motherboard problems are quite serious and can easily prevent your PC from starting. When a PC refuses to start (and the power supply checks out properly), you should suspect a problem with the motherboard or its CPU, memory, or cache. Fortunately, motherboards are tested by the BIOS each time you start the PC, so it is a relatively simple matter to pinpoint the failure.

Drive system

All computers need some form of permanent storage. Although the memory on your motherboard holds files and programs while the system is running, there must be some form(s) of storage while the power is turned off. Most contemporary systems use three drives: a 3.5-in *floppy drive,* a *hard drive,* and a *Compact Disk Read-Only Memory* (CD-ROM) *drive.* You will also need a *drive controller.* The drive controller may be incorporated onto the motherboard itself or can be included as an expansion board plugged into a motherboard expansion slot.

We always seem to need more storage, so drive upgrades are some of the most interesting and diverse upgrades available. The upgrade options range from adding a second hard drive or a CD-ROM drive to installing SCSI drives, tape drives, and other removable media drives like SyQuest and Iomega drives. The choice of upgrade really depends on your particular needs. If you just need local storage, a new hard drive will usually work out well. If you want to protect your work, adding a backup tape drive is advisable. If you're taking work from system to system, an Iomega Jaz, or Zip drive might be just the thing. If you feel

the need to create your own multimedia presentations, a CD recorder might be the ticket. Now that
Digital Versatile Disc (DVD) drives are becoming
available, those will likely be the next *hot* upgrade
(replacing existing CD-ROM drives).

Computers rely on the hard drive or floppy drive
(and now the CD-ROM drive) to load an operating system (OS) before you're able to use a PC, so drive problems—especially with the hard drive—can halt your
operating system and prevent you from accessing the
system. This also means your files on the drive will
remain inaccessible. When you do find a defective
drive, your only option is to recover and back up as
many files as possible (if possible) and then replace
the drive outright. In actual practice, you'll find that a
great deal of your troubleshooting is going to center
around drives and drive problems.

Video system

You will also need a means of displaying text and
graphics, so a video system is definitely a major
requirement. The video system requires a *video controller* and a *monitor*. The video controller may be
incorporated onto the motherboard itself or can be
included as an expansion board plugged into a motherboard expansion slot. The monitor is your "window"
(no Microsoft pun intended) into the PC, and monitors
are available in an astounding array of styles, sizes,
and features.

Video has always been a data-intensive operation
and has traditionally presented a bottleneck. Even
with the advanced motherboard buses available today
and new technologies like video acceleration and 3-D,
video performance remains challenged by the constant
demand for ever-increasing screen resolution and
color depth. As a result, upgrading an existing video
board will almost always yield a noticeable improvement in system performance.

Video systems run "hot and cold" when it comes to troubleshooting. If the video board fails outright or is not installed properly in its bus slot, the system won't start at all (usually indicated by a series of beeps and no display). In this case, your only course is to check the video board's installation and replace the video board if necessary. However, you're going to find that most video problems under Windows 95 are driver-related. These are less catastrophic problems, but they can be tricky to figure out.

Sound board

Virtually all PCs today use a high-quality Sound Blaster-compatible stereo sound board with full-range (20 hertz, or Hz, to 20 kilohertz, or kHz) *powered speakers*. Given the rapid evolution of sound technology, few motherboards incorporate sound hardware. So you'll need to add a sound board to a motherboard expansion slot. Sound boards also offer other features such as CD-ROM drive interfaces, joystick ports, and MIDI ports that can further enhance the system.

As it happens, sound board upgrading is not as popular a procedure as you might imagine. Once a sound board is installed and operational, there are typically few compelling reasons to go through the hassle of replacing it. The two main reasons for upgrading a sound board are to replace a defective unit and to upgrade a related feature of the sound board (i.e., to replace the sound board's proprietary CD-ROM interface with a standard IDE interface).

From a troubleshooting standpoint, sound boards have truly become a nest of trouble for technicians—most often during initial installation and upgrade. Today, sound boards are packed with features, and each of those features demands resources (interrupts, I/O addresses, and DMA channels) from the PC. As a consequence, sound boards are prime candidates for hardware conflicts. In addition, you must worry about microphone cables, speaker cables, and CD signal and audio cables. Finally, sound boards demand several different multimedia drivers, which must be installed properly—and *replaced* if the sound board is ever changed to a different model. In short, you can expect sound boards to present more than their fair share of problems.

I/O ports

You'll need some parallel and serial ports. The *parallel ports* are used to operate printers—as well as other parallel port devices like Iomega or SyQuest drives. *Serial ports* can also operate printers, but it's much more common to use serial ports for a mouse and external modem. In most cases, you'll usually find one parallel port and two serial ports incorporated right onto the motherboard itself. If not, you can always add some ports with an I/O expansion board plugged into a motherboard expansion slot.

Game port

If you plan to play games such as flight simulators, you'll need a game system made up of a *game port* and a *joystick*. Motherboards never provide a game port, but sound boards usually do. You could also add a stand-alone game port card in a motherboard expansion slot or add an I/O board that includes a game port. The main issue here is that there can only be *one* game port in the system, so make sure that only one game port is enabled. All others should be disabled.

Mouse and keyboard

Finally, you'll need input devices—a means of entering commands and making selections. A *mouse* and a *keyboard* are the two classic input devices. In most cases, they are fast and simple to add or replace, although mice and other pointing devices (like a

GlidePoint touch pointing device) require individual drivers. Mice and keyboards are available in a wide array of types and styles, so feel free to shop around.

Cases and Power Supplies

Now that you've seen an overview of the required parts, we can get to the good stuff—choosing the specific parts for your PC. Let's start off with cases and power supplies and then work into a discussion about the motherboard. There aren't too many things to buy, but you *do* need to consider the important issues for each component. We won't talk about troubleshooting much more until we actually get into the assembly process.

Cases

The *case* is usually one of those items that get left until the very end (or is treated as an afterthought). In fact, the case should be one of your *first* considerations. Your choice of case will define how many drives you can install, how large a power supply you use, how big the motherboard can be—and the number of expansion slots available. There are three general classifications of case: baby, desktop, and tower.

The *baby case* lives up to its name. It is a small desktop case that fits an absolute minimum of items. You're usually limited to two drives because the 130- to 175-W power supply is typically located right behind the drives, and there's no room left for an internally mounted hard drive. You are also limited to using a small motherboard—typically with a minimum of features or ports. Finally, you have very few expansion slots to work with. The bottom line with a baby desktop case is that you really limit your options and expandability. The only real reason you'd choose a baby case is when you only need a minimum system, and desktop space is at a premium.

Desktop cases come in a variety of shapes and sizes and generally offer a lot more versatility and upgrade potential than baby cases. With regular desktop cases, you can usually count on two external and two internal drive bays—great for a floppy drive, CD-ROM, and one or two hard drives. If you find a desktop case with three external drive bays, you can even add a tape drive. The other advantages to regular desktop cases is that they have the physical space to support larger power supplies (usually 200 to 250 W), fit larger motherboards, and support more expansion boards. If you have any inclination to expand your system, a desktop case will give you few headaches.

The *tower case* is typically a large vertically mounted case that is designed to hold the maximum number of drives. There are often four or more external drive bays and at least four internal drive bays. The extra space also allows the largest power supplies (300 + W), which are vital to support an array of different drives. Tower cases can hold the very largest of motherboards (although in practice the motherboards are rarely larger than those found in a regular desktop). Tower cases also provide the best air ventilation and can have three or more fans and air filters. The other advantage of good air flow is that high-end CPUs (even multiprocessor motherboards) can be cooled most effectively. On the down side, tower cases are the most expensive. They are placed on the floor, so cabling to a mouse, keyboard, monitor, and other sound equipment can be strained. Tower cases are usually reserved for only the most serious system builder.

The importance of drive bays.   One of the most important aspects of a case is the number of drive bays it provides. There are two types of drive bays: external and internal. *External drive* bays are open to the outside of the case. Floppy drives, CD-ROM drives, and tape drives all require external drive bays. *Internal drive* bays are mounting frames located inside of the case. Typically, only hard drives use internal drive bays. As a minimum, your case should have two external drive bays (for a floppy drive and CD-ROM) and one internal drive bay (for the hard drive). If you have additional drive bays, you will have room for expansion.

Fitting power supplies and motherboards. You also need to remember that your case will have to hold a power supply and motherboard—these things will actually have to *mount* to the case, so be sure that your power supply and motherboard have ample space and mounting points for a clean fit. There's nothing more frustrating than getting that new motherboard home and finding out that it won't fit in the case (or the mounting holes don't line up). Fortunately, cases are often offered with built-in power supplies, so that's one less headache to deal with. If you are upgrading to a new (typically larger) case, it may also help you to get a case and matched power supply. The new power supply should offer more power capacity than your original one, and you will probably have an easier time getting rid of or reusing the old case if it has a working power supply with it.

Mechanical specifications. Given the problems matching motherboards, cases, and power supplies, the computer industry has responded by developing a series of physical specifications (or *form factors*) for the construction of motherboards, cases, and power supplies. The idea is that power supplies, motherboards, and cases all built to a certain specification will fit correctly without the problems of mixing and matching. The three most popular specifications are Baby Advanced Technology (AT), ATX, and NLX.

The *Baby AT* "specification" is really a bit of a misnomer. There is no formal standard, but Baby AT motherboards and cases have been around for years. Even so, there were often problems getting motherboards, cases, and power supplies to fit together. Many times, the CPU and heat sink/fan were located in the front of the Baby AT motherboard in front of the expansion slots and would interfere with some full-slot expansion boards.

The *ATX* specification (now at version 2.01) was really the first mass-market specification to embrace the development of standard-sized motherboards, power supplies, and cases. The ATX form factor is essentially a Baby AT motherboard rotated 90 degrees within the chassis enclosure using a new mounting configuration for the power supply. In this way, the CPU is placed away from the expansion slots (off to the right of the expansion slots), allowing the slots all to hold full-length expansion cards. ATX defines a double-height aperture to the rear of the chassis that can be used to host a wide range of on-board I/O ports. Only the size and position of this aperture are defined, allowing PC manufacturers to add new I/O features to their systems.

By comparison, the *NLX* specification (now version 1.2) is slanted toward a low-profile PC with easier access to components for upgrade or replacement. NLX is supposed to support current and future processor technologies, as well as the Accelerated Graphics Port (AGP) for high-performance graphics. NLX is also supposed to support "tall memory" technology and provide more system-level design and integration flexibility. For example, the NLX expansion cards are in a "riser card" off the motherboard, the CPU is located at the front left of the motherboard, tall components are located away from expansion boards, and I/O ports are stacked to support more available connectors.

As a result of these mechanical specifications, choosing standard parts can simplify your assembly quite a bit. You can get more information on ATX specification at www.teleport.com/~atx/ or on the NLX specification at www.teleport.com/~nlx/.

Case manufacturers.   There are actually dozens of quality PC case manufacturers around the world. The list below indicates just a few of the better-known manufacturers. You can find a complete list of ATX case makers at www.teleport.com/~atx/chas/index.htm.

Amtrade Products	www.amtrade.com
Enlight	www.enlightcorp.com.tw
Fong Kai Industrial	www.fkusa.com
InWin Development	www.in-win.com
ProCase	www.procase.com.tw/68.htm

Power supplies

Your next issue is choosing the power supply. Whether you're upgrading or building from scratch, do yourself a favor and *don't* skimp on the power supply. Buy plenty of power, and go with a reputable manufacturer—marginal power supplies will cause no end of trouble with erratic system operation and premature failures. Power is measured in watts. Each device in the computer demands power, so there must be enough power available from the power supply to run the motherboard, the drives, and all of the expansion boards in your system. Don't be afraid to buy power—it's OK to have too much. It's when there isn't enough that you have problems. If you go with a desktop case, plan on a 200- to 250-W power supply. For tower cases (with lots of drives), go with a 300- to 350-W unit.

If you really want to apply some numbers when estimating the size for a power supply, you can use the 150 + 12 rule. This is a baseline of 150 W for the motherboard and CPU and then 12 W for every drive and expansion board you plan to add. So if you want a system with a floppy drive, hard drive, CD-ROM, modem board, and video board, figure on 150 + 12 + 12 + 12 + 12 + 12, or 210 W. If you buy a 220- to 250-W power supply, you'll have plenty of power, although your upgrade options may be a bit limited.

Power connectors.   When you look at the power supply, you'll notice two different sets of cables. One set plugs into the motherboard. The other set of cables provides power to each drive. There must be enough drive power cables to run each drive in your system. Otherwise, you'll need Y cables to split power. In practice, these Y cables should be avoided, so the more drive power cables, the better off you'll be. As a rule, the more wattage offered by the power supply, the more drive cables that are available.

There are two well-accepted sets of cables to power the motherboard: a Baby AT configuration, shown in Fig. 1.1, and the ATX configuration, shown in Fig. 1.2.

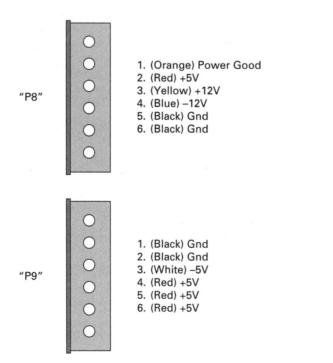

"P8"

1. (Orange) Power Good
2. (Red) +5V
3. (Yellow) +12V
4. (Blue) –12V
5. (Black) Gnd
6. (Black) Gnd

"P9"

1. (Black) Gnd
2. (Black) Gnd
3. (White) –5V
4. (Red) +5V
5. (Red) +5V
6. (Red) +5V

Figure 1.1   Power connections for a Baby AT power supply and motherboard.

1. +3.3V	11. +3.3V
2. +3.3V	12. −12V
3. Gnd	13. Gnd
4. +5V	14. PW_ON#
5. Gnd	15. Gnd
6. +5V	16. Gnd
7. Gnd	17. Gnd
8. PWRGD	18. −5V
(Power Good)	19. +5V
9. +5V SB	20. +5V
(Standby for RTC)	
10. +12V	

Figure 1.2 Power connections for an ATX power supply and motherboard.

The classic Baby AT configuration uses two 6-pin Molex connectors (usually marked P8 and P9) that are inserted adjacent to each other. The rule here is black wires together. A Baby AT power supply provides four voltage levels (+5 volts, or V, −5 V, + 12 V, and −12 V) along with a power good signal. The ATX power supply uses a slightly different 20-pin single-connector scheme that includes a + 3.3-V power supply along with the other conventional voltages. It is important to stress that Baby AT power supply connectors will not mate with an ATX motherboard (and vice versa).

Mounting points. Of course, you'll actually have to mount that power supply into the case. This can get a little bit sticky with Baby AT systems because nobody tells the case makers and the power supply makers to put their screw holes in the same places. So unless you plan on using Crazy Glue, you should make sure that the power supply will mount properly in the case. If you can find a case with a suitable power supply already mounted, that might take some of the guess-work out of your assembly. Also remember that you'll need to turn the power supply on and off. This means the case has to have a hole for the power switch, as well as the AC line cord and fuse opening. Remember that ATX- and NLX-style cases and power supplies should be easier to match.

Choosing a power supply for upgrade or replacement. Power supplies are some of the most overlooked parts of a PC—probably because you never see them in operation the way you do with video boards or hard drives. Also, once a power supply is operating, there is really no reason to replace it unless you have to replace a defective unit or want to support more devices that were added during a PC upgrade.

Choosing an upgrade for an existing power supply follows the main rules that we have already covered; the power supply needs to provide adequate power to the computer, it needs to fit in the physical space available, it needs to mount properly and securely, and it should have an ample number of drive power cables available without having to resort to Y cables. Once again, *buy from a reputable manufacturer.* Although all power supplies perform the same basic jobs, they are *not* all created equal. Go with a manufacturer that uses top-quality parts in a well-designed and reliable power supply that is backed with a strong warranty and friendly return policy. The best PC components in the world cannot make up for a poor power supply.

Power supply manufacturers. When you're ready to shop, check out some of the power supply makers below, or check out the complete list of ATX power supply makers at www.teleport.com/~atx/powe/index.htm.

Astec America	www.astec.com
NMB Technologies	www.nmbtech.com
PC Power & Cooling	www.pcpowercooling.com
Phihong USA	www.phihongusa.com
PowerOn	www.power-on.com

Motherboards and Related Parts

The motherboard is the heart and soul of your computer. Motherboards and the components on it will define the capabilities (and limitations) of your system. This part of the chapter covers the major elements of a motherboard and shows you the points to consider. Table 1.1 lists the specifications for the example motherboard shown in Fig. 1.3.

TABLE 1.1 Specifications for the Intel PD440FX Motherboard

Element	Specification
Form factor	ATX form factor
Expansion slots	Two ISA slots, three PCI slots
Microprocessor	Single Pentium II processor operating at 233 or 266 MHz Slot 1 processor connector 256- or 512-kbyte L2 cache on the substrate in the SEC cartridge
Main memory	Four 72-pin SIMM sockets Support for up to 256 Mbytes of EDO memory Support for nonparity, parity, or ECC DRAM
Chipset and PCI/IDE interface	Intel 82440FX PCI chipset Integrated PCI bus mastering controller Two fast IDE interfaces Support for up to four IDE drives or devices Support for two USB interfaces
I/O features	National PC87307VUL Super I/O controller Integrates standard I/O functions: floppy drive interface, one multimode parallel port, two FIFO serial ports, real-time clock, keyboard and mouse controller, IrDA-compatible interface
Other features	Intel/AMI BIOS Plug-and-Play compatible Advanced Power Management

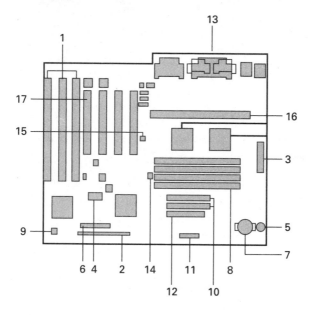

1. ISA connectors
2. Front panel header
3. ATX Power connector
4. Flash BIOS IC
5. Speaker connector
6. Configuration jumper block
7. Battery
8. SIMM sockets
9. Fan 1 header
10. IDE connectors
11. General Purpose I/O header
12. Floppy drive connector
13. Back panel I/O connectors
14. Hard disk LED (HDD LED) header
15. Fan 2 header
16. Slot 1 processor connector
17. PCI connectors

Figure 1.3 Connection diagram for a typical mother-board.

Form factor

The dimensions and mounting points for the motherboard are typically defined by the form factor, and this
is often the first specification you see when evaluating
the new motherboard. Your choices are generally Baby
AT, ATX, or NLX. The dimensions for a typical ATX
motherboard are illustrated in Fig. 1.4. The form factor may not be the most exciting motherboard issue
when compared to CPUs and chipsets, but you need to
understand it right up front—all the processing power
in the world won't do you much good if the motherboard doesn't fit in the case.

Expansion slots and buses

Motherboards alone rarely offer all of the features
that you need for your computer. Fortunately, you can
add other devices to the motherboard by plugging

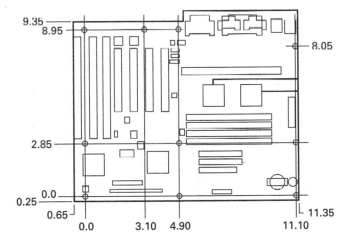

Fig 1-4

Figure 1.4 ATX motherboard dimensions.

them into *expansion slots* or *buses*. There are five different architectures that you should be familiar with: ISA, VLB, PCI, AGP, and USB. Virtually all new motherboards offer some (or all) of these buses, and the capabilities of your new system will largely be defined by the buses that are available on your particular motherboard. These bus types are defined below:

ISA.   This is the classic Industry Standard Architecture (ISA) 16-bit 8.3-MHz expansion bus. Although it offers limited data throughput and resources when compared to other buses, you'll still find plenty of 16-bit cards, such as modems, Small Computer Systems Interface (SCSI) adapters, and sound cards. Your motherboard should have three to five ISA slots on board. Some of the newest Pentium II motherboards (like Intel's PD440FX) only offer two ISA slots. That might be enough for a modem and sound card but leaves no additional ISA slots for future expansion.

VLB.   The Video Local Bus (VLB or VL bus) was originally designed by the Video Electronics Standards Association (VESA) as a high-performance 32-bit video expansion bus that could support improved video under Windows without the performance bottleneck imposed by ISA slots. The VLB works well, and you will find video boards and drive controllers designed for VLB slots. However, the VLB is tied to clock speed, and new motherboards can have problems supporting VLB properly. There can also be problems when motherboards try to support both VLB and PCI buses together. As a rule, you should avoid VLB motherboards unless you get a deal you just can't refuse.

PCI.   The Peripheral Component Interconnect (PCI) bus originally evolved as a 32/64-bit answer to the VLB. Where the VLB is generally geared toward video systems, the PCI bus is designed to support general-purpose devices (although video boards and drive controllers are the most common). PCI is generally a better-performing bus with superior data throughput. Its fixed 33-MHz clock speed makes PCI much more stable than VLB, and its bus mastering features make it ideal for high-performance devices. Your best bet is usually to find a motherboard with two or three PCI bus slots on it.

AGP.   Video continues to be a bottleneck for cutting-edge graphics applications which push video resolution, color depth, and image complexity to the limit (especially for video and real-time 3-D images). The AGP is a high-performance port using a superset of PCI architecture designed to handle huge volumes of video data. Where the 32-bit PCI bus implementation can handle 133 megabytes per second (Mbytes/s), the 32-bit implementation of an AGP can handle 533 Mbytes, and future implementations of AGP are expected to handle 1 gigabyte per second (Gbytes per second) of video data and higher. This opens up whole new possibilities for games and visualization software. However, you will require AGP support in the motherboard's PCI chipset and in the BIOS and operating system. Microsoft is likely to support AGP in the next major releases of Windows 95 (code named "Memphis") and Windows NT (version 5.0). Until then, AGP will not have a significant impact on your system.

USB.   Expanding a PC has always been a hassle—setting jumpers and DIP switches often leads to hardware conflicts that cause system crashes and lockups. Plug-and-Play (PnP) technology has helped ease the burden of installations and upgrades to some extent, but adding new devices remains troublesome. The Universal Serial Bus (or USB) is a relatively new architecture that allows you to add devices outside of the PC simply by daisy chaining devices together without worrying about resource allocation. The devices can also be installed and removed while the system is running (called *hot insertion and removal*). USB is slanted primarily toward external devices such as monitors, joysticks, keyboards, and so on.

The number of slots.   One of the most frustrating choices a PC user can make is which card to remove when there aren't enough expansion slots. Do yourself a favor and get plenty of slots on your new motherboard. Generally, five ISA slots and three PCI slots will give you a great range of expandability. If you're using a small case (and small motherboard) and don't plan to do much expansion, you can get away with fewer slots.

CPU support

The CPU is the main processing component on your system. All program instructions and data are eventually processed through the CPU. The faster and more powerful a CPU is, the more performance your computer will offer. Keep in mind that a CPU also has to operate in conjunction with other elements of the motherboard, so a newer CPU installed into an older motherboard may not offer the same performance as a new CPU installed in a state-of-the-art motherboard. When selecting a CPU, always make sure that your motherboard will support it. In virtually all cases, the motherboard (or system) documentation will list the CPUs that are compatible with the motherboard. For example, the Intel PD440FX motherboard will support a Pentium II CPU operating at 233 or 266 MHz, but the Tyan Titan III supports Pentiums from 75 to 166 MHz. Improved CPUs are one of the most popular upgrades for a motherboard, so choose your motherboard to accommodate the CPUs that you may choose to add in the future. Otherwise, you'll find yourself having to replace the entire motherboard outright.

You can select from among several different types of CPUs. We could easily write a book explaining the specifications and technologies behind the current CPUs, but we'll just mention some high points of each type. Some leading candidates are outlined below.

Intel processors. Intel (www.intel.com) originated the CPU and has held the lead in CPU design ever since. Although intense competition (especially from Advanced Micro Devices, or AMD) has eroded Intel's hold on the CPU market, they remain a leader in reliable, high-performance CPUs.

- *Pentium Classic.* This is really the current CPU for general-purpose end-user computers. Available at clock speeds from 66 to 200 MHz, the Pentium represents your best trade-off between cost and performance. If you can afford a 133-MHz CPU or higher, your investment will be well rewarded.

- *PentiumPro.* The PentiumPro is a version of the Pentium that has been optimized to operate at higher clock speeds (200+ MHz) and to support high-performance 32-bit operating systems and networking environments such as Windows NT as well as Symmetric Multiprocessing (SMP). If you need a Windows NT system, you might consider the PentiumPro; otherwise, stick with the Pentium Classic.

- *Pentium MMX (P55C).* The Multimedia Extension (MMX) is a redesign of the Pentium to provide a better data processing and higher performance, and it is particularly well suited for processing intensive applications such as networking, graphics, MPEG (Motion Picture Experts Group) video playback, and so on. The MMX will work with DOS, Windows, OS/2, and Unix, but it uses split voltages (2.8 and 3.3 V). To use a "true" MMX CPU, you'll need a motherboard that is designed with an MMXcompliant chipset. Otherwise, you can get a Pentium OverDrive CPU with MMX for your Pentium Classic motherboard. Now that companies like Tyan (www.tyan.com) and Supermicro (www.supermicro.com) are releasing motherboards for true MMX CPUs, these may prove the more appealing (but more expensive) option.

- *Pentium II (Klamath).* The Pentium II (formerly called Klamath) represents a shift in traditional CPU design. Rather than a traditional chip, the Pentium II is a module based on the PentiumPro design, but it offers external improvements that are not in the chip itself. The CPU plugs into a slot (called Slot 1) rather than a socket. Again, the Pentium II is another high-performance CPU for Windows NT and networking systems, so you probably won't want to run right out and buy one unless you're planning some high-end processing work.

AMD processors. AMD, once an ally of Intel, has become its most serious competitor (www.amd.com). AMD CPUs have had very few compatibility problems, offer excellent performance, and have been priced *very* competitively in relation to Intel CPUs. The problem with AMD is that their CPUs are not quite as fast as Intel's (AMD CPUs are just now pushing to 166 MHz), although this margin is also narrowing.

- *5×86.* This 32-bit CPU put AMD on the map, and the 5×86 provided Pentium-class compatibility for older 486 CPU upgrades. If you want to nudge some extra life out of your 486, consider dropping a 5×86/133 in there.

- *K5.* The K5 is AMDs answer to the Pentium, and although its clock speeds are bit slower, the K5 performs on par with Pentiums of the same speed. One of the attractive benefits of the K5 is its extremely low price. If you want a good CPU and don't need a current Intel speed demon, AMD may provide a good alternative.

- *K6.*   The next-generation AMD CPU is the K6. AMD is banking on using MMX technology, as well as technology from NexGen (which AMD acquired). If the last few years are any indication, the K6 will be an important competitor to Intel's P55C MMX processor. The K6 should be shipping now and should be in broad use by the time you read this book.

Cyrix processors.   Cyrix (www.cyrix.com) has worked hard to catch AMD and Intel, and its efforts have paid off with several of their recent CPUs. However, Cyrix has also been plagued by incompatibilities between their CPUs and some Intel-based motherboard chipsets. If you choose a Cyrix CPU, be *very* certain that it has been certified to work properly with the motherboard and operating system you plan to use.

- *6×86 (M1).*   The 6×86 (or M1, as it was called before) is a strong alternative to the Intel Pentium and is able to outclass the Pentium in some respects. However, you must be sure that the 6×86 will operate properly at the motherboard's rated bus speed and chipsets. The math coprocessor feature of the 6×86 is also considered behind the Pentium, so math-intensive applications (i.e., Quake) will not run nearly as well with the 6×86. The 6×86 also runs *hot,* so get the newer 6×86L (low-power) version or plan on the very best heat sink/fan you can find.

- *M2.*   The next generation of the 6×86 will incorporate many of the MMX improvements promised by the Intel P55C. Cyrix expects to double the performance of the 6×86 and to resolve the heating and math coprocessor issues that have plagued them in the past. The 6×86 will be available by late 1997.

Heat sinks and fans. CPUs also run hot—*very* hot. If you don't want to ruin your CPU investment, you'll need to think about ways to keep the CPU cool. As a rule, use a heat sink/CPU fan that mounts directly to the CPU itself. The heat sink is basically a metal radiator that carries heat away from the CPU. The fan—built right into the heat sink—forces air through the heat sink, which makes the cooling process much more efficient. You can typically buy a heat sink/fan when buying the CPU.

There is a lot of variation in the quality of heat sink/fans. Often, inexpensive (a.k.a. cheap) fans will fail early and take your CPU with them. Because you can't see or hear the heat sink/fan, you won't know if it stops working until you're opening the PC to replace a failed CPU. Spend a few extra dollars and get a good-quality heat sink/fan (the fan should be a ball bearing type).

CPU voltages. Power means heat. By reducing the voltage used to drive the CPU, you reduce the heat that CPU generates—the CPU runs cooler. The traditional 5-V CPUs have been replaced by 3.5-, 3.3-, and even 2.8-V devices. The other advantage to low-power devices is that they save electricity. However, you must be sure that the motherboard is providing the *right* voltage to the CPU. If the voltage is too high, you can burn the CPU out (or at least keep it running warmer than it needs to be). If the voltage is too low, the CPU may function erratically or not work at all. This is even more complicated with the new generation of MMX CPUs (regardless of manufacturer), which use *two* voltages (2.8 and 3.3 V) instead of one.

There are two means of controlling CPU voltages: a motherboard voltage jumper and a CPU voltage regulator. If your motherboard has a built-in regulator, you can set a jumper on the motherboard to select the proper voltage. If your motherboard does not have an on-board regulator, you can place a CPU regulator *between* the CPU and socket. The CPU regulator just acts as a secondary socket. When selecting a CPU regulator, make sure to choose a unit with plenty of power-handling capacity. Remember that those regulators are going to get hot too, so a higher-capacity regulator will run cooler and more reliably.

Selecting clock speeds and multipliers. Most motherboards today are designed to accept several different types of CPUs (i.e., a Pentium 90, 100, 120, 133, 166, 200, or 233). However, the motherboard must know which CPU is installed and what clock speed to operate the CPU at. For today's motherboards, you are concerned with two settings: the clock speed and the multiplier. The *clock speed* can generally be set at increments from 40 to 66 MHz (this is often called the system bus speed or just bus speed). For example, the Tyan Titan III can be set to 50, 60, or 66 MHz. The *multiplier* is the required setting to boost the bus speed to the appropriate speed for the CPU. For example, to run a 120-MHz Pentium, you need to set a clock speed of 60 MHz, and a multiplier of 2×. After you set these jumpers properly, you can install the CPU in the socket. Typical multipliers are 1×, 1.5×, 2×, 2.5×, and 3×.

CPU upgrades. Upgrading a CPU is not difficult, but it can be confusing if you don't know the rules. CPU compatibility is limited by your motherboard, so check with your motherboard manual (or the manual that came with your system) to see exactly what CPUs and clock speeds are supported. For example, you just can't stuff a Pentium 166 into your 486SX/25 motherboard. You also can't use an MMX CPU in your conventional Pentium motherboard. Although motherboards are much more versatile today, CPUs are *not* universal, and there *are* limits on the range of CPUs that will work with your particular motherboard. Voltage is another concern. Current CPUs are all low-voltage devices, but there are different classes of low-voltage such as 3.5, 3.3, and 2.8 V. Make sure that you choose a CPU with a voltage rating that will match your motherboard, or plan on adding the proper voltage regulator module.

Incorrect speed and multiplier settings are common problems when upgrading a CPU. If you forget to adjust the motherboard (or set the jumpers incorrectly), you may encounter poor performance, or the system may not operate at all. If you fail to set the CPU voltage correctly (or neglect to install a voltage regulator), you may permanently damage the CPU.

Main memory (RAM) support

All computers need memory to hold program data and instructions while the CPU is executing them, so Random Access Memory (RAM) is needed on the motherboard. Older motherboards usually incorporated 1 or 2 Mbytes of RAM on the motherboard and then allowed you to add more memory in the form of SIMMs. Today, many motherboards use SIMMs exclusively. This makes it much easier to replace defective memory without having to replace the entire motherboard. You generally choose some preinstalled amount of RAM when you select your motherboard.

RAM types

There are *many* types of RAM available for the PC, but we'll take a look at a few of the more common types below:

- *DRAM (Dynamic RAM).* This is the basic workhorse memory. Cheap and reliable, you can get adequate performance from simple DRAM. All motherboards support ordinary DRAM, although performance is often limited compared to advanced forms of memory. Today, DRAM is frequently found in video boards. Keep in mind that the generic term *DRAM* is often (incorrectly) applied to other forms of memory.

- *EDO RAM.* Extended Data Output RAM uses specialized motherboard chipsets to take advantage of the particular timing offered by EDO RAM. The EDO feature of the RAM allows the CPU to access data once its available from the RAM rather than having to make the CPU wait until the data is ready. This results in about a 5 percent performance improvement for the system. You *can* use EDO RAM in a non-EDO-compatible motherboard, but there will be no performance improvement.

- *BEDO RAM.* The *Burst Extended Data Output RAM* (as the name already implies) reads data in a burst. After a valid address has been provided, the next three data locations are read in only *one* clock cycle each. This can dramatically increase the apparent speed at which a CPU reads memory. This RAM type is presently supported by the VIA chipsets 580VP, 590VP, 680VP. The main downside of BEDO RAM seems to be an inability to cope with bus speeds faster than 66 MHz.

- *FPM RAM.* Fast Page Mode RAM uses a slightly different method of internal addressing that allows the RAM to find related or nearby pieces of data faster (concurrent pieces of data that are on the same memory "page"). This results in improved performance for the system but costs slightly more. Your motherboard must also be capable of supporting FPM RAM.

- *SDRAM.* Synchronous DRAM is a relatively new type of enhanced memory that allows data to be transferred at *any* point in the system's clock cycle rather than just at certain points. This makes for faster overall memory performance. SDRAM can also "burst" large amounts of data to and from memory. Only the newest motherboard chipsets support SDRAM.

- *SRAM.* Static RAM is *very* fast memory (down to 10 to 15 nanoseconds, or ns), but it is too complex and expensive for main storage (i.e., 16 to 32 Mbytes of main memory). Instead, SRAM is used for the system's memory *cache* (128 to 512 kbytes). Caching improves the system's performance by allowing frequently used data to be stored in very fast memory, which is local to the CPU.

SIMM specifications. When you purchase memory, you'll need to understand how memory is specified. SIMMs are measured by four attributes, pin count, size, speed, and parity:

- *Pin count* is the size of the SIMM device. There are 30-pin SIMMs (1 byte wide) and 72-pin SIMMs (4 bytes wide). For today's CPUs and motherboards, you will almost certainly use 72-pin SIMMs. An emerging memory device that you will probably encounter is the Dual Inline Memory Module (DIMM) with 168 pins.

- *Size* is generally the number of megabytes provided on the SIMM. A 2Mx32-bit SIMM yields (2M×4 bytes) 8 Mbytes of memory. A 4M×32-bit SIMM yields (4M×4 bytes) 16 Mbytes of memory, and so on. As you will note below, parity bits are not included in the size determination of any memory device.

- *Speed* is the access speed of the memory (rated in nanoseconds). Smaller speed numbers mean faster memory, and this is desirable. For Pentium-type systems, you will probably use 60-ns memory or faster. Memory *must* be fast enough to suit the CPU; otherwise, data will be lost, and errors will be generated.

- *Parity* is a byte-level form of error checking that allows the motherboard to catch single-bit errors when reading from memory. A parity bit is added to every *byte* in RAM (so a 2M×32 SIMM would have 4 bytes only—no parity—and a 2M×36 SIMM would have 4 extra bits for parity). The motherboard calculates a parity bit for the byte read and then compares that bit against the parity bit read from memory. If the parity bits match, the byte is assumed to be good, and the system moves along. If they do not, an error is flagged and the system halts. If you have the choice between parity and nonparity RAM, go with parity RAM.

Filling a memory bank.   Memory is organized into *banks*. A bank must have enough data bits to cover the CPU's data bus. For example, a Pentium CPU uses a 64-bit data bus. This means that a memory bank must be 64 bits "wide." Because one 72-pin SIMM provides 32 bits of data, you will need two 72-pin SIMMs to fill one complete bank. If there are six 72-pin SIMM slots on the motherboard, you have three banks to work with. If there are four 72-pin SIMM slots on the motherboard, you have two banks to work with, and so on. When you add RAM to a motherboard, you *must* add enough SIMMs to fill a complete bank.

> **NOTE:** Don't worry if you're still not clear on the above explanations—the concept memory banks is one of the most troublesome PC concepts to master.

Cache RAM.   Your motherboard will also need cache RAM to enhance system performance. You will use SRAM as the cache, and it is usually added to the motherboard as Dual Inline Package (DIP) Integrated Circuits (ICs) rather than as SIMMs. Another popular form of cache is the cache on a stick (COAST) module. A COAST module resembles a SIMM and plugs into a socket in the motherboard. Get at least 256 kbytes of cache for your motherboard; 512 kbytes is better, but the performance jump from 256 to 512 kbytes is not so great.

Cache basically works by keeping frequently used instructions and data in a small amount of very fast memory. This way, the contents of cache can be accessed by the CPU much faster than it could be from main memory. The popular wisdom states that if a little cache is good, *more* cache must be better. The problem is that adding more cache can be a significant expense, and the performance improvement is not proportional to your upgrade. For example, moving from 128 kbytes of cache to 256 kbytes offers a dramatic performance improvement. Moving from 256 to 512 kbytes of cache provides some additional improvement but not as much as moving from 128 to 256 kbytes. Moving from 512 kbytes to 1 Mbyte adds some more benefit but not as much as moving from 256 to 512 kbytes and not nearly as much as moving from 128 to 256 kbytes. As a rule, plan on at least 256 kbytes of cache if your PC has 8 to 16 Mbytes of main RAM. If the PC has 16 to 64 Mbytes of RAM, go for 512 kbytes of cache; over 64 Mbytes of main RAM, get 1 Mbyte of cache.

Getting enough RAM.   Pick up at least 8 Mbytes of RAM for your system (i.e., two 1MBx32-bit SIMMs). This is really a minimum if you have any hope of ever running Windows 95. In most cases 16 Mbytes (i.e., two 2MBx32-bit SIMMs) is considered the nominal amount of RAM for Windows 95. If you can afford it, go for 32 Mbytes of RAM.

Upgrading memory.   Memory upgrades are extremely popular, especially these days when memory costs are so low. When adding memory, there are four issues to consider: type, size, speed, and parity.

1. All your memory should be the same type (i.e., EDO or FPM). If you already have EDO memory in your system, you would be best off adding more EDO memory. Whenever you mix memory types, you run the risk of some system compatibility issues. If you *must* mix memory types for any reason, try not to mix types within the same bank.

2. Check your motherboard's documentation carefully to see what combinations of memory sizes will fit in each bank. We like to think that we can add as much memory as we want wherever we want it, so long as an entire bank is filled. Unfortunately, this is not always the case, and many motherboards limit the sizes of SIMMs or DIMMs that it will support. Avoid using double-sided SIMMs if you can help it (the term *double sided* simply refers to the way the SIMM is addressed, not whether there are ICs on both sides of the SIMM).

3. The speed of your new memory (in nanoseconds) should match the speed of your existing memory. For 486 systems, 70-ns memory was usually enough. For Pentium systems, 50 to 60-ns memory is preferred. Slower memory *will* work, but you'll need to add wait states in the Complementary Metal-Oxide SemiConductor CMOS Setup that force the CPU to wait until the memory catches up (this ruins your system performance). If you do use memory that is *slightly* slower than other memory in your system, place the slower memory in bank 0.

4. Finally, check the parity of your existing memory. Parity is a simple means of memory error checking designed to find single-bit errors. If your current memory uses parity (any size x9 or x36, such as 2Mx36), you should add only parity-type memory. If you add nonparity memory, you'll have to disable the parity-checking feature through CMOS Setup or a motherboard jumper. If you are currently

using nonparity memory, you could add either parity or nonparity memory, but you cannot enable parity checking.

> **NOTE:** I strongly encourage the use of parity or an alternate error-detection/correction technique (such as Error Correction Code, or ECC). Error checking does not improve system reliability as such, but it can prevent errors from going undetected and possibly causing system lockups, crashes, and data corruption.

Memory manufacturers.   You will frequently get additional memory from a motherboard maker or computer superstore like CompUSA, but check out these on-line resources: Kingston Technology at www.kingston.com and PNY at www.pny.com. You might also like to look at an interesting page on memory from Micron at www.micron.com/mti/marketing/htmls/buyersnews/bn 296.html.

BIOS support

The Basic Input/Output System (BIOS) is a form of permanent memory that holds the instructions that your motherboard hardware needs to communicate with the operating system. In short, BIOS "drives" your motherboard hardware and supports features such as PnP, power conservation, and specialized buses like the USB. BIOS is provided *with* the motherboard, so you don't have to select it separately, but you may choose to upgrade the BIOS later on.

Normally, BIOS should only be upgraded when there is a clear problem with the BIOS that prevents an important feature or function from working or if a BIOS upgrade would expand the capabilities of your hardware. For example, suppose you're using a motherboard video system and you decide to upgrade the video system by adding a new video board. You'd need to disable the motherboard video system. Some poorly designed motherboards may be unable to fully disable their on-board video because of a flaw in the BIOS, and an upgrade might fix the problem. As another example, some older motherboards needed a BIOS upgrade to support the AMD 5×86 and K5 or the Cyrix 6×86. It would not be a surprise to see a few motherboards require a BIOS upgrade to support newer third-party CPUs such as the AMD K6 or the Cyrix M2.

Traditionally, BIOS upgrades required you to replace the actual BIOS Read-Only Memory (ROM) on the motherboard. But today, virtually all BIOS uses "flash" ROM ICs, which can be reprogrammed "on the fly" without having to replace the actual BIOS IC.

Contrary to popular belief, BIOS can fail. This is a rare problem, but it is always a possibility. In most cases, BIOS faults are detected early during the Power-On Self-Test (POST) when the BIOS checksum is tested. If the checksum calculated during the POST does not match the checksum value stored in the BIOS, an error is generated. You can detect the BIOS error using a POST reader card. The real problem with BIOS faults is that the system simply won't start until the BIOS IC is replaced, so the PC can be out of commission until a BIOS is installed. The corrupt BIOS cannot be reprogrammed because the system won't boot in order to start the flash routine.

BIOS makers.   If you want to explore the features of modern BIOS or examine the issues involved in potential upgrades, take a look at any of the major BIOS makers below:

American Megatrends (AMI)	www.megatrends.com
Award Software International	www.award.com
MicroFirmware, Inc.	www.firmware.com
Microid Research	www.mrbios.com
Phoenix Technologies, Ltd.	www.ptltd.com

Chipsets and controllers

In the early days of PCs, motherboards were built with hundreds of discrete logic ICs (just take a look at any original IBM PC/AT). It didn't take long for designers to realize that the major PC functions could be condensed onto Application-Specific ICs (ASICs). Not only did this philosophy reduce the total number of ICs needed to build a motherboard, but it also allowed performance to improve, and it reduced the power demands and costs of a motherboard. Eventually, IC design evolved to the point where all the major features needed for a motherboard could be provided with just a couple of related (and very complex) ICs. These related ICs became known as *chipsets*. Modern motherboard capabilities are largely defined by their chipset. In fact, most chipsets are specific to certain CPU families. Table 1.2 illustrates a technical comparison between several of the most popular chipsets. It is not necessary for you to understand all of the technical issues in Table 1.2; simply understand that there are subtle differences between chipsets. When shopping for a motherboard, you will probably encounter the following chipsets.

Pentium motherboards have these chipsets:

- Intel 430FX (Triton)
- Intel 430HX (Triton 2)
- Intel 430VX
- Intel 430TX
- VIA Apollo VP-1
- VIA Apollo VP-2
- VIA Apollo VPX
- SIS 5571
- Very Large-Scale Integration (VLSI) Lynx
- Opti Viper-M

TABLE 1.2 Compression Between the Intel FX/HX/VX and the VIA Apollo VP-1/VP-2 Chipsets

	Intel 430FX	Intel 430HX	Intel 430VX	VIA VP-1	VIA VP-2
Chipset package					
IC package	208×2	324×1	208×2	208×2	324×1
No. of chips	100×2	201×1	100×2	100×2	201×1
CPU type					
Dual processor	No	Yes	No	No	No
75-MHz bus speed	No	No	No	Yes	Yes
Expansion bus					
ISA	Yes	Yes	Yes	Yes	Yes
EISA	No	Yes	No	No	No
2d-level cache					
Asynchronous SRAM	Yes	No	Yes	Yes	No
Burst SRAM	Yes	No	Yes	Yes	Yes
Pipelined burst SRAM	Yes	Yes	Yes	Yes	Yes
Maximum cache	512 kbytes	512 kbytes	512 kbytes	2048 kbytes	2048 kbytes
Maximum cacheable DRAM	64 Mbytes	64/512 Mbytes	64 Mbytes	64/512 Mbytes	64/512 Mbytes
DRAM					
FPM and EDO mixed	Yes	Yes	Yes	Yes	Yes
BEDO RAM	No	No	No	Yes	Yes
SDRAM	No	No	Yes	Yes	Yes
5V/3V	Yes	Yes	Yes	Yes	Yes
Maximum memory size	128 Mbytes	512 Mbytes	128 Mbytes	512 Mbytes	512 Mbytes

TABLE 1.2 Compression Between the Intel FX/HX/VX and the VIA Apollo VP-1/VP-2 Chipsets (Continued)

	Intel 430FX	Intel 430HX	Intel 430VX	VIA VP-1	VIA VP-2
DRAM (Cont.)					
Read timings (60/66)	7222/7222	4222/5222	5222/6222	4222/5222	4222/5222
w/EDO	N/A	N/A	6111/7111	4111/5111	4111/5111
w/SDRAM/BEDO	N/A	N/A	6111/7111	4111/5111	4111/5111
Single-write PH	X333	X222	X222	X222	X222
Bursts	N/A	N/A	X111	X111	X111
w/EDO	Yes	Yes	Yes	Yes	Yes
w/BEDO/SDRAM	Yes	Yes	Yes	Yes	Yes
Asymmetric DRAM	RAS-Only	CAS before RAS	CAS before RAS	CAS before RAS	CAS before RAS
Smart refresh	4QW	8QW/merge	4QW	16QW/merge	16QW/merge
Refresh type	Dynamic	Predictive	Dynamic	Predictive	Predictive
CPU write buffer	Dynamic	Predictive	Dynamic	Predictive	Predictive
Paging algorithm	No	Dynamic	No	Dynamic	Dynamic
64-Mbit technology	No	Yes	No	No	Yes
Parity support	No	Yes	No	No	Yes
ECC support	No	Yes	No	No	Yes
Programmable MA/WE					
Driving capability	No	Yes	?	?	?
PCI bus					
PCI 2.1	No	Yes	Yes	Yes	Yes
Asynchronous PCI Interface possible?	No	No	No	Yes	No

42

	100 Mbyte/s	>100 Mbyte/s	>100 Mbyte/s	132 Mbyte/s	132 Mbyte/s
Throughput	100 Mbyte/s	>100 Mbyte/s	>100 Mbyte/s	132 Mbyte/s	132 Mbyte/s
Four PCI masters	Yes	Yes	Yes	Yes	Yes
CPU-to-PCI buffers	4DW	6DW	5DW	5DW	5DW
PCI-to-DRAM posting	12DW	20DW	18DW	64DW	64DW
PCI-to-DRAM prefetch	No	22DW	10DW	32DW	32DW
Maximum burst length	4 kbyte	4 kbyte	4 kbyte	4 kbyte	4 kbyte
Snoop ahead	Yes	Yes/pipelined	Yes	Yes/pipelined	Yes/pipelined
Writeback policy	Write/read	Merge/forward	Merge/forward	Merge/forward	Merge/forward
Arbitration					
Passive release	No	Yes	Yes	Yes	Yes
MTT	No	Yes	Yes	Yes	Yes
PIIX3/USB	No	Yes	Yes	Yes	Yes
Latency enhancements	No	Yes	Yes	Yes	Yes
PCI concurrency					
DRAM prefetch	No	Yes	Yes	Yes	Yes
During PCI reads	No	Yes	Yes	Yes	Yes
Writeback	No	Yes	Yes	Yes	Yes
Merge and forward	No	Yes	Yes	Yes	Yes
PCI/CPU	No	Yes	Yes	Yes	Yes
Grant during pass	N/A	Yes	Yes	Yes	Yes
Plug-and-Play					
DMA type F	Yes	Yes	Yes	Yes	Yes
One programmable	Yes	Yes	Yes	Yes	Yes
CS steerable	Yes	Yes	Yes	Yes	Yes

TABLE 1.2 Compression Between the Intel FX/HX/VX and the VIA Apollo VP-1/VP-2 Chipsets (Continued)

	Intel 430FX	Intel 430HX	Intel 430VX	VIA VP-1	VIA VP-2
Plug-and-Play (*Continued*)					
DMA channels	Yes	No	Yes	Yes	Yes
Steerable IRQs	Yes	No	Yes	Yes	Yes
Integrated I/O					
Extension to ATA-33					
(33-Mbyte/s transfer rate)	No	No	No	Yes	Yes
PIO/master	Yes	Yes	Yes	Yes	Yes
Two channels	Yes	Yes	Yes	Yes	Yes
Independent drive timing	No	Yes	No	?	?
USB	No	Yes	Yes	Yes	Yes

For PentiumPro motherboards, these chipsets are available:

- Intel 440FX (Natoma)
- Intel 440LX
- Intel 450GX/KX (Orion)
- VIA 680 VP Apollo P6

There is only one popular chipset for the Pentium II (Klamath) motherboards: the Intel 440LX.

> **NOTE:** There are other chipsets that you will encounter, but these are the most popular ones.

Chipset makers. If you want more detailed information on chipsets and their capabilities, you can check with the following major chipset makers directly:

Intel	www.intel.com
OPTi	www.opti.com
SIS	www.sisworld.com
VIA	www.via.com.tw

Motherboard ports. Your motherboard is going to need several different ports in order to communicate with the "outside world":

- *Serial ports.* Get a motherboard with two serial ports. One serial port is usually for a serial mouse, and the other serial port is typically for an external modem. If your motherboard does not offer serial ports, you can add them by installing a multi-Input/Output (I/O) card into an available expansion slot.

- *Parallel ports.* If you plan to use a printer, at least one parallel port will be a necessity. Virtually all motherboards provide one parallel port. If your motherboard does not offer a parallel port, you can add one by installing a multi-I/O card into an available expansion slot.

- *Keyboard port.* This is really a no-brainer. There has to be a connector on the motherboard to accept the input from a keyboard. The keyboard port may be soldered directly to the motherboard itself, or there may be a cable header from the motherboard to a keyboard connector at the case.

- *Mouse port.* Although you can easily install a serial mouse on an existing serial port, you may choose to get a motherboard with a built-in PS/2 mouse port. This frees up the second serial port for other uses (such as a serial printer). Keep in mind that some motherboards will require a small adapter cable to connect a PS/2 header on the motherboard to a PS/2 connector in the case.

On-board controllers. Many of today's motherboards incorporate video and drive controllers. This adds convenience to the motherboard because it saves two expansion slots (one for the video controller and one for the drive controller). If you choose to upgrade the video and drive controller later, you can always disable the motherboard controllers and install the replacement controllers as expansion boards.

- *Floppy drive controllers (FDC).* You will find a 34-pin Insulation Displacement Connector (IDC) header (a.k.a. ribbon cable connector) on the motherboard for your floppy drives (usually labeled FDD). The floppy drive port will support two floppy drives (A: and B:) and can be disabled through a jumper on the motherboard. If you install a drive controller expansion board later, you will need to disable the floppy drive port.

- *Hard drive controllers (HDC).* You will probably find two 40-pin IDC headers (a.k.a. ribbon cable connectors) on the motherboard for your hard drives (usually labeled primary HDD and secondary HDD). The primary hard drive port should support

two EIDE hard drives (C: and D:). The secondary
hard drive port should support two ordinary IDE
devices (usually E: and F:), although one of those
secondary devices is often an ATAPI (AT attachment
packet interface) IDE CD-ROM drive. If you install a
drive controller expansion board later, you will need
to disable these hard drive ports.

■ *Video controllers.* Your motherboard will probably
offer a 15-pin high-density Super Video Graphics
Array (SVGA) connector and 1 or 2 Mbytes of video
RAM. This allows you to connect your monitor
directly to the motherboard. If you need higher resolutions, color depths, more video memory, or better
overall video performance, you can always disable
the motherboard video system and install a video
controller expansion board later on.

Choosing a motherboard upgrade

There are two key reasons why you would upgrade
your motherboard assembly: (1) your current motherboard has reached the limits of its usefulness and you
can no longer improve performance with motherboard
add-ons or other system devices or (2) you want to take
advantage of a feature or bus that is not available on
your current motherboard (i.e., a USB or PCI bus).

The next issue to consider is the motherboard's own
upgradeability. Once you install the new motherboard,
ask yourself how far you'll be able to upgrade it. A
low-cost, low-end motherboard may be a temporary
plus for your system, but it may become obsolete in
just a few months. When selecting a new motherboard, strike a balance between price and versatility.

Motherboard manufacturers. Selecting a motherboard
for your new or existing system is perhaps the single
most important choice you can make. Table 1.3 presents you with a listing of motherboard vendors, each

TABLE 1.3 On-Line Index of Motherboard Manufacturers

Manufacturer	Internet address
ABIT Computer	www.abit.com.tw
Acer	www.acer.com
AIR	www.airwebs.com
AMI	www.megatrends.com
AOpen	www.aopen.com.tw
Asus	asustek.asus.com.tw
A-Trend	www.atrend.com
BCM	www.bcmcom.com
BEK Computer	www.bek-tronic.com
BioStar Group	www.biostar.net
Chaintech	www.chaintech.com.tw
Diamond Flower	www.dfi.com.tw
DTK	www.gan.net/dtk/main.html
Elitegroup	www.ecsusa.com
EPOX	www.epox.com
FIC	www.fic.com.tw
Free Computer Tech	www.freetech.com
Gemlight Computer	www.gemlight.com.hk
Gigabyte	www.giga-byte.com
GVC	www.gvc.com.tw
Intel	www.intel.com/design/motherbd
I-Will	www.iwill.com.tw
J-Bond	www.jbond.com
JDR Microdevices (HK) Ltd.	www.2themax.com
Joss Technology	http://josstech.com
Micronics	www.micronics.com
MicroStar	www.msi.com.tw
Mitac	http://mitac.mic.com.tw/index.html
M Technology	www.mtiusa.com
Octek	www.oceanhk.com
QDI	www.qdigrp.com
Shuttle	www.shuttlegroup.com
Soltek Computer	www.soltek.com.tw
Soyo	www.soyo.com
Sun Microelectronics	www.sun.com:80/sparc/ SPARCengineUltraAX/
SuperMicro	www.supermicro.com
Taiwan My Comp	www.mycomp-tmc.com/
Taken Corporation	www.taken.com.tw
Tekram	www.tekram.com
Tyan	www.tyan.com

with a selection of products for every requirement and budget. Take your time to compare specifications and prices.

Video System

Your new PC is going to need a video system to display the text, graphics, and multimedia images associated with everyday computing. A video system generally consists of two elements: the video controller and the monitor. This part of the chapter explains the issues involved with a typical video system and shows you some important considerations in choosing the right parts.

Video controllers

Next to your motherboard, the video controller is your most important choice. Indirectly, the video controller defines the visualization capabilities of your PC. With the intense interest in multimedia, video, and computer graphics, video systems are evolving at an incredible rate. The advantage of a motherboard-based video controller is convenience—you save money and need only plug a monitor into the motherboard's video connector. However, motherboard video controllers are limited in terms of memory and sophistication, and they cannot be upgraded without replacing the motherboard or installing a stand-alone video board. If you do not have a video controller already available on your motherboard (or wish to install a more powerful video system), you will have to install a stand-alone video board in a motherboard expansion slot. If you choose a motherboard with PCI slots, *definitely* get a PCI video board for top performance.

Resolutions and color depth.   Video boards are rated in terms of their resolution and color depth. The *resolution* is the number of pixels that can be displayed on a monitor. Resolution is usually rated in terms of width times height (i.e., 640×480). *Color depth* is the number of colors that can be displayed at a given resolution. Most current video boards can support resolutions up to 1024×768 at color depths of 16 or 256 colors. More advanced video boards can support 65K colors or even 16M colors. As a rule, Windows 95 will work well with 800×600 resolution at 256 colors, but if you're considering the use of a DVD drive for MPEG-2 video, you should go for a video board that will support a minimum of 800×600 resolution in High Color (65K color) mode.

Table 1.4 illustrates the capabilities of a typical high-end video board. For each standard resolution, you can see the various color depths that the board can handle. Note that color depths are often expressed as bits per pixel (or bits/pixel). Below each bits/pixel entry is the amount of video memory available. Note that more video memory allows higher resolutions and color depths. The relationship of bits to colors is as follows: 8 bits yield 265 colors, 16 bits support 65K colors, 24 bits provide 16M colors (called *True Color* mode), and 32 bits supply an astounding 4 billion colors.

Video memory. As you probably noticed in Table 1.4, video memory holds the data that composes your

TABLE 1.4 Typical Video Resolution and Pixel Depth

Resolution	Bits/pixel		
	2 Mbytes	4 Mbytes	8 Mbytes
640 × 480	8, 16, 24, 32	8, 16, 24, 32	8, 16, 24, 32
800 × 600	8, 16, 24, 32	8, 16, 24, 32	8, 16, 24, 32
1024 × 768	8, 16	8, 16, 24, 32	8, 16, 24, 32
1152 × 864	8, 16	8, 16, 24, 32	8, 16, 24, 32
1280 × 1024	8	8, 16, 24	8, 16, 24, 32
1600 × 1200	8	8, 16	8, 16, 24

image. Higher resolutions and color depths require more video memory. The actual formula for memory is total pixels × bits/pixel." Suppose you have an 800×600 image at 16 bits/pixel (65K colors). That's (800×600) 480,000 pixels. You would need (480,000×16) 7,680,000 bits (960,000 bytes, or 960 kbytes) of video memory to show one complete image on the screen. As a rule, select a video board with at *least* 1 Mbyte of video memory. But today, 2-Mbyte video boards are quite inexpensive. If you're planning on a high-end 3-D video board, plan on 4 Mbytes of video RAM.

Video BIOS. All video boards running above 640×480 ×16 require the use of video drivers to support higher resolutions and color depths. Although protected-mode drivers for Windows 95 can easily support a wide range of enhanced video modes, this presents some unique problems for DOS applications (especially games). When you select a video board, make sure that the video BIOS supports VESA 2.0 extensions or later. This will eliminate the need for DOS VESA drivers. If you're using an older video board without VESA support in BIOS, try the Universal VESA display driver available from SciTech Software, Inc., at www.scitechsoft.com. Some game manufacturers also distribute the Universal VESA driver in their technical support web site.

Windows drivers. Don't even think of buying a video board unless it comes with the very latest video drivers for Windows 95. Older Windows 3.1 video drivers will *not* work well with Windows 95. Another issue to consider is driver age. Video drivers are some of the most frequently updated items, and you can usually find a video driver update on the video card manufacturer's technical support web site. If you're installing a used video board that's a few years old, be sure to check for the latest drivers first.

Choosing a video upgrade. Video systems have always been somewhat of a bottleneck in terms of processing. A new video board can go a long way toward improving your system's performance. Choose a PCI video board with graphic acceleration and a minimum of 2 Mbytes of video memory. This will place you head and shoulders above older ISA video boards and will dramatically improve video. If you work with three-dimensional (3-D) rendering or graphics at all, tack on high-speed 3-D acceleration to your specifications (and a total of 4 Mbytes of video memory if you can afford it). If your current video system is integrated onto the motherboard, you should have a clear picture of *exactly* how to disable the motherboard video *before* proceeding with the upgrade.

Normally, video boards do not utilize an interrupt, but some high-end video boards *will* use one. Before installing a new video board, determine if it uses an interrupt, and make sure that the interrupt is not being used by any other devices in the system. Otherwise, you'll need to reconfigure the video board to an unused interrupt.

Video board manufacturers. Some of the most popular and well-respected video board manufacturers are shown below. Take some time to compare the features and performance of each video board before you make a purchase.

ATI Technologies	www.atitech.ca
Diamond Multimedia	www.diamondmm.com
Matrox	www.matrox.com
Orchid Technology	www.orchid.com
STB	www.stb.com

Monitors

The video controller drives your monitor, which actually displays the video image. In a sense, the monitor

is your "window" into the PC. Choose a monitor with
care. A poor-quality monitor can ruin the finest video
image. You should select a 15- to 17-in SVGA monitor
with a dot spacing (or pitch) of .30 or less (preferably
.28 or less). If you work with computers extensively,
you should consider spending the extra money for a
20- or 21-in monitor. Larger monitors support higher
resolutions and allow you to "zoom" documents and
drawings with far more clarity than you could achieve
with a smaller monitor (in short, larger monitors can
keep you from going blind). You should also make sure
that the monitor is *noninterlaced*. Interlaced monitors
tend to show more flicker and cause more eye fatigue.
You will notice that the monitor's signal cable has a
15-pin high-density connector on the end that will fit
perfectly with the connector on your video board. We
won't talk much about monitor specifications or
attributes because you won't be *building* the monitor,
and you can actually use any compatible monitor to
test the newly built system.

Monitor manufacturers.   There are many monitor manufacturers and many *good* monitors. If you can actually try out a monitor before buying it, please take
advantage of that opportunity.

Nanao	www.traveller.com
Nokia	www.nokia.com
Radius, Inc.	www.radius.com
Viewsonic	www.viewsonic.com

Sound boards

Originally driven by the needs of game developers,
sound boards evolved as a replacement for the obnox-
ious beeping and tweeting of a PC speaker. Over the
last 10 years, sound has become a prominent feature
of virtually all new systems. Today, good-quality
sound boards provide efficient sound file playback,

extremely precise sound synthesis, and orchestral quality music. Whether you plan to play audio Compact Discs (CDs), use the newest games, or make multimedia presentations, you will almost certainly want some sound in your new computer.

Sound issues

Unless you're a real audiophile, you probably won't be able to detect a significant sound difference between good-quality sound cards, so feel free to compare prices. Still, there are some issues to consider when you're shopping for new or upgrade sound hardware, as discussed below.

CD-ROM interfaces. Many sound boards come with a CD-ROM drive port already incorporated. If you plan to attach a CD-ROM to the sound board, make sure that the port is compatible with your CD-ROM drive. Older sound boards provided several proprietary CD-ROM ports (i.e., Sony, Panasonic, and Mitsumi), but that has largely been abandoned by major sound cards in favor of a standard ATAPI IDE port (the same interface used for hard drives). If you have the choice, get an IDE port on your sound card rather than a proprietary port. This gives you the option of connecting the CD-ROM drive to the sound board or to the secondary hard drive port. It also allows you to upgrade your CD-ROM drive later without having to worry about interface compatibility.

MIDI/game port. You'll also probably notice a 15-pin connector on the sound board. This is the Musical Instrument Digital Interface (MIDI) port. If you have a MIDI instrument, you can connect it to the sound board and compose your own music. If you're as "musically challenged" as I am, you can switch the MIDI port to serve as a standard joystick port. You can enable or disable the game port through a jumper on the sound board. If you already have another game port (or multi-I/O card) in the system, you can leave the port disabled.

MIDI memory. High-end sound boards (such as the Sound Blaster AWE32) often provide SIMM slots for additional memory. This is MIDI memory and is used when composing MIDI music or taking sound samples. If you're not going to be composing music, don't bother buying extra memory for the sound board.

CD audio connector. When selecting a sound board, look for the CD audio connector. It's a small four-pin connector usually located at the top of the sound board roughly in the middle. You'll run a thin, four-wire cable between the CD-ROM audio output and the sound board—this is how you get your favorite CD to play through your sound board's speakers. If there is no CD audio connector, you'll have to run a patch cable from the CD-ROM drive's headphone output to the sound card's line input and then adjust the sound board's mixer to set the correct CD audio level.

Speakers. You'll also need to buy some powered speakers for the sound board. Do yourself a favor and spend a few extra dollars for some decently powered speakers capable of a wide frequency range. Cheap speakers can sound "tinny" and can ruin the output of any sound board. If you have a choice, avoid battery-powered speakers (unless you can afford a regular stream of new batteries). Another compelling argument for good speakers is the use of DVD drives and MPEG-2 decoder boards. DVD-Video movies and presentations will soon be available, and good speakers will make the most of DVD sound.

Sound board manufacturers. You have several major sound board manufacturers to choose from today, and they all offer high-quality symphonic sound and MIDI music capability:

Creative Labs	www.creaf.com
Ensoniq	www.ensoniq.com
Turtle Beach	www.tbeach.com

Drive Systems

You're going to need a selection of drives to round out your new PC. Drives serve two vital purposes. First, drives provide permanent storage for your programs and files (including the operating system). Second, drives allow for the convenient and economical distribution or exchange of programs and files. In most cases, you're going to use a minimum of three drives: a floppy drive, a hard drive, and a CD-ROM drive. However, there are other drives which you should also be familiar with. This part of the chapter explores the various drives that you will commonly encounter and will cover the essential points that you should be aware of.

Drive controllers

It is quite common for a motherboard to provide two drive controller ports and one floppy controller port. If so, you do not need to use a drive controller. If your motherboard does not offer an on-board drive controller, you *will* need to add one in an available expansion slot. The drive controller should support up to two EIDE hard drives on a *primary* controller port (C: and D:) and up to two more EIDE/IDE devices on a *secondary* controller port (E: and F:). The controller should also support two floppy drives (A: and B:). If your motherboard has PCI bus slots, you should certainly get a PCI drive controller for best performance. But if you're building PCs out of older bits and pieces, you can use an ISA drive controller board with its own on-board BIOS to supplement the older motherboard's BIOS.

EIDE support. Your drive controller *must* support EIDE hard drives (high-performance drives with storage capacities over 528 Mbytes). The drive controller may have an on-board BIOS for supporting EIDE, but if your motherboard BIOS already supports EIDE, you can disable the controller's on-board BIOS. Another advantage of EIDE drives and controllers is a superior data transfer rate. Look for PIO Mode 3 (~13 Mbytes/s) or PIO Mode 4 (~16 Mbytes/s) data transfer rates in your drive controller and hard drives.

Drive controller manufacturers. Due to the popularity of motherboard-based drive controllers, there are few manufacturers of EIDE controllers. However, the manufacturers that specialize in stand-alone EIDE controllers generally offer some outstanding products. Take a look at some of the manufacturers below:

Crest Microsystems	www.crestor.com
DTC Products	www.datatechnology.com/products/products.htm
Promise Technology	www.promise.com

SCSI controllers

Now is a good time to bring up the subject of SCSI controllers. SCSI is a "bus-type" system that allows numerous different devices to all share a common signal bus cable. SCSI hard drives, SCSI CD-ROM drives, SCSI tape drives, SCSI scanners, SCSI Zip or Jaz drives, and numerous other SCSI devices can all coexist and share a single SCSI bus. In fact, most drives can be obtained with an SCSI interface rather than an EIDE interface. Whereas many motherboards support the EIDE interface, few support a native SCSI interface. If you plan to support SCSI devices in your new

PC, you'll almost certainly need to add a SCSI controller board to the system.

If you use a motherboard with PCI bus slots, be sure to use a PCI SCSI controller for optimum performance. Keep in mind that installing an SCSI controller will demand system resources (namely, an Interrupt Request (IRQ) and some amount of I/O space, as well as space for the SCSI BIOS). Another major issue with SCSI is "termination"—both ends of a signal cable must be properly terminated, or none of the SCSI devices may function properly. Termination is certainly not difficult, but it can be tricky to master, and termination oversights are one of the most frequent causes of SCSI installation and upgrade problems.

SCSI and EIDE.   Contrary to popular belief, SCSI and EIDE interfaces can coexist. It is certainly possible to have EIDE hard drives and an SCSI scanner and CD-ROM or an ATAPI CD-ROM with two SCSI hard drives or EIDE and SCSI hard drives, and so on. The trick is that your system will try to boot from EIDE drives *first*. In other words, if you have an EIDE and an SCSI hard drive in the same system, the EIDE drive will traditionally be the boot device. However, late-model SCSI controllers are starting to offer an option that will override the EIDE boot device and allow an SCSI drive to boot the system even if there is an EIDE drive present (this is a feature of the latest SCSI BIOS versions).

SCSI versus EIDE.   Even though EIDE and SCSI devices will work together (so long as there are no hardware conflicts between the SCSI and EIDE controllers), the question of which is better remains. The line between SCSI and EIDE has grown a bit murky over the last few years. It used to be that if you needed very large drives and top performance, you stuck with SCSI. Today, Advanced SC5 + Programming Interface, or ASPI, (SCSI) and ATAPI (EIDE) devices share remarkably similar performance characteristics. Although SCSI hard drives can still outsize EIDE drives by several gigabytes, that gap is closing too. Both are *fine* interfaces, but you need to make your choice based the advantages and disadvantages of each interface.

SCSI only requires one controller to handle up to seven SCSI devices (such as hard drives, tape drives, scanners, and so on). All these devices can be connected to the same SCSI signal bus. As a result, the hardware and cabling requirements are simpler. When you deal with SCSI, you also need to deal with drivers. You need an ASPI driver for the SCSI controller and all other SCSI devices in your system (except for hard drives, which are handled by the SCSI BIOS). This can be a problem if you install protected-mode drivers for Windows 95 and then need to use the devices under the Disk Operating System (DOS). On the other hand, installing real-mode drivers for DOS can interfere with Windows 95's operation. Finally, not all SCSI devices are equally compatible with every SCSI controller. For example, if you replace your SCSI controller with one of a different make and model, you'll need to install a whole new set of drivers and probably will even have to reformat your SCSI hard drives.

By comparison, EIDE offers its own set of challenges. Most EIDE controllers provide one fast EIDE channel and one slower IDE channel—both channels can only support two devices. You usually put the fast devices (your hard drives) on the EIDE channel and put the slower devices (your CD-ROM, older IDE drives, or IDE tape drive) on the IDE channel. This complicates the installation and cabling a bit, and you may run into trouble mixing slow and fast devices (i.e., CD-ROM drives and hard drives) on the same channel. However, EIDE devices are readily available and can be as much as several hundred dollars cheaper than their SCSI counterparts. EIDE is also supported directly in BIOS, so you don't need drivers to

run the EIDE interface (although you still need
ATAPI drivers for some devices such as CD-ROM
drives). This makes EIDE equally robust under DOS
and Windows 95.

In short, EIDE is the choice when price is your top
concern and you won't need to expand your system
very much. SCSI is the way to go when you need the
very best multitasking performance and capacity and
you plan to add a large number of devices to the system (such as building your own Windows NT server).

SCSI BIOS.   SCSI BIOS is required in order to operate
SCSI hard drives. If you have SCSI hard drives in
your system, you'll need to have the SCSI BIOS
enabled. Keep in mind that the SCSI BIOS will occupy
space in the Upper Memory Area (UMA) along with
the motherboard BIOS, video BIOS, and any other
BIOS in the system. If you need an SCSI controller
for things like a scanner, and there are no SCSI hard
drives, you can almost always disable the SCSI BIOS.

SCSI drivers.   Drivers are another important SCSI
issue. The SCSI controller and all other SCSI devices
(except for hard drives) use drivers. You'll need real-
mode drivers to operate the SCSI system under DOS
and protected-mode drivers to run your SCSI devices
under Windows 95. Drivers are always provided with
the respective SCSI device, but always make it a point
to keep your SCSI drivers updated. The latest SCSI
drivers are typically available for download from each
particular SCSI manufacturer.

SCSI controller manufacturers.   Unlike EIDE controllers, there is a real proliferation of SCSI controllers in the marketplace. A few of the more notable
SCSI controller manufacturers are listed below:

Adaptec   www.adaptec.com
AdvanSys   http://advansys.com/prod.htm

Bus Logic   www.buslogic.com
Q Logic   www.qlc.com

Floppy drives

Floppy drives are the classical "removable media," and disks remain a simple and convenient means of distributing simple software or moving files between PCs. Your drive controller will support up to two floppy drives (A: and B: drives). You will need a 34-pin ribbon cable to attach your floppy drive(s) to the drive controller. Today, all you really need is one 3.5 in floppy drive, although you can get "dual" drives (a 3.5- and 5.25-in drive in the same drive assembly).

Floppy cable.   Take a look at the floppy drive cable. You'll notice that there is a single 34-pin connector at one end and two 34-pin connectors at the other. The end with the single connector attaches to the drive controller, the "middle" connector attaches to drive B:, and the end-most connector attaches to drive A:. The cable should not exceed about 2 ft (around 60 cm) in length.

Floppy jumpers.   If you look closely, you'll also notice that the floppy drive probably has several jumpers. These jumpers serve several purposes, but as a general rule, you should *not* move them. Most floppy drives are jumpered as drive B:; that's OK. The little twist you see between the two drive connectors on your floppy cable converts the end-most drive back to A:.

Floppy drive manufacturers.   Floppy drives are readily available and very inexpensive. The two most popular floppy drive manufacturers are shown below:

Teac   www.teac.com
Mitsumi   www.mitsumi.com

Hard drives

The hard drive is really the center of your mass-storage strategy. The media is not removable, but hard drives provide huge amounts of very fast storage. Your EIDE drive controller will typically support up to two EIDE drives and up to two IDE devices, so plan on at least one EIDE hard drive (~2.1 Gbytes or larger) on the EIDE channel. If you use an ATAPI IDE CD-ROM, you can place it on the IDE channel. Drive prices drop so fast that you can get very large drives for a reasonable price.

Hard drive cable.   Take a look at the hard drive cable. You'll notice that there is one 40-pin connector at one end and two 40-pin connectors at the other. The end with the single connector plugs into the drive controller, and the other connectors plug into the drives. Unlike floppy drive cables, the hard drive cable has no effect on drive letter assignments. SCSI cables may look like EIDE cables at first glance, but SCSI cables have either 50 or 68 pins.

Drive jumpers.   IDE/EIDE hard drives use jumpers to define their relationship. Drives can be set as the primary drive (master) or the secondary drive (slave). A primary and secondary drive can be installed on each of the two drive channels, so the controller can support up to four drives. The first drive installed on the first (EIDE) channel should be jumpered as the primary drive (this will be C:). The second drive installed on the first (EIDE) channel should be jumpered as the secondary drive (this will be D:). The first drive installed on the second (IDE) channel should be jumpered as the primary drive (this will be E:), and the second drive installed on the second (IDE) channel should be jumpered as the secondary drive (this will be F:). As a rule, do *not* use the cable select (CS) jumper option if one is available.

SCSI devices are identified in a slightly different manner using eight Identification (ID) numbers (0 to 7). The SCSI controller is typically assigned ID7, and the first two SCSI hard drives are usually given ID0 (the boot drive) and ID1. Other SCSI devices use the remaining SCSI IDs. All SCSI IDs are selected with jumpers.

Drive parameters. When installing a hard drive, you will need to configure the drive's parameters in the system's CMOS Setup. Parameters usually include cylinders, sectors/track, heads, landing zone, and write precompensation. Table 1.5 compares the parameters of several popular hard drives. We won't go into the specifics of each parameter here, but you'll need to locate those parameters in the drive's documentation and be sure to record them for future reference. If your BIOS and drives support autodetection (virtually all EIDE implementations *do*), you may be able to get away with autodetecting the hard drive rather than entering specific parameters.

Hard drive manufacturers. Hard drives are some of the most rapidly evolving devices for the PC. Compare products, specifications, and warranties among the major drive makers below:

TABLE 1.5 Comparison of Popular Hard Drive Parameters

Drive model	Cylinders	Heads	Write Precomp position	Landing Zone	Sectors	Megabytes (gigabytes)
AC11200	2484	16	0	0	63	1281 (1.2)
72025AP	3936	16	0	0	63	1937 (1.9)
72577AP	4996	16	0	0	63	2459 (2.4)
72700AP	5248	16	0	0	63	2583 (2.5)
AC33100	6136	16	0	0	63	3166 (3.1)
AC34000	7752	16	0	0	63	4001 (4.0)

Maxtor	www.maxtor.com
Quantum	www.quantum.com
Seagate	www.seagate.com
Western Digital	www.wdc.com

CD-ROM drives

Most major software packages are now distributed on CD and are even partially run from the CD. As a consequence, CD-ROM drives have emerged as an absolute necessity in the modern computer. The typical CD-ROM drive is an inexpensive and reliable device that requires almost no maintenance. More recently, CD-ROM drives have become "bootable," although you need a suitable drive, BIOS, and bootable CD media to make use of this feature. Plan on at least one CD-ROM drive for your new system.

CD-ROM drives are rated in terms of *seek time* and *transfer speed*. Seek time—the time required to locate desired information—can be as much as 100 or 200 milliseconds (ms). Transfer speed—the rate at which data is transferred from the drive to the interface—is a multiple of the original floppy drive transfer speed of 150 kbytes/s. For example, a 2X CD transfers data at 300 kbytes/s, a 4X CD transfers data at 600 kbytes/s, and so on. Today, you can get 8X and 10X drives at very reasonable prices, and 12X and 16X versions are readily available. With the recent emergence of DVD technology, it is unlikely that CD-ROM drives will become much faster.

CD-ROM interfaces.   Older CD-ROM drives used any one of several proprietary interfaces (i.e., Mitsumi and Panasonic). That worked with multimedia kits, where the drive's controller was integrated into the sound board. If you didn't have a controller handy, though, you were stuck. Today, most major CD-ROM drives offer an ATAPI IDE interface that is exactly the same interface as your hard drive. You can then install the

CD-ROM with any IDE drive controller. If you have a secondary channel on your drive controller, an ATAPI IDE CD-ROM drive is a perfect fit. As a rule, never install a hard drive and CD-ROM drive together on the same channel.

> **NOTE:** The very latest CD-ROM drives are being fitted with PIO Mode 3 and PIO Mode 4 capability. This does not improve their slow data transfers, but it does make it possible for them to coexist on the same channel with fast EIDE hard drives.

CD audio.   If you want to play CD audio through your sound board, you will need to connect the audio output of your CD-ROM drive to your sound board through a thin, four-wire audio cable. Make sure that the CD-ROM drive comes with a suitable connector for CD audio. Remember, unless you buy the CD-ROM and sound board together as a multimedia kit, you may have to buy the CD audio cable separately.

CD-ROM manufacturers.   There is surprisingly little difference between CD-ROM drives other than their overall seek time and transfer speed, but feel free to browse some the major CD-ROM manufacturers for more tidbits of information:

Hi-Val	www.hival.com
Mitsumi	www.mitsumi.com
Plextor	www.plextor.com

DVD drives

Today, the CD-ROM is showing its age, and a single CD no longer provides enough storage for the increasing demands of data-intensive applications. A new generation of high-density optical storage called DVD is now appearing. DVD stands for several different things. In the early phase of DVD development, it stood for Digital Video Disc. Later on, it stood for

Digital Versatile Disc (because it could hold programs and data as well as video and sound). Regardless of what you call it, DVD technology promises to supply up to 17 Gbytes of removable optical storage on your desktop PC. In addition, the DVD drive is fully backward-compatible with CD audio, CD-ROM, CD-I, and other popular CD formats, so the DVD can actually replace your existing CD-ROM drive. The only standard that DVD cannot currently support is CD-R (Recordable CDs).

DVD interfaces and jumpers.   DVD drives are now available with either SCSI or EIDE interfaces, so no proprietary interface card is required. This simplifies installation quite a bit. The EIDE version can easily coexist as a secondary (slave) drive with your existing hard drive on the same controller channel (unlike older CD-ROM drives, which could interfere with high-performance data transfers). You could also place the DVD drive on a secondary EIDE channel. Jumpers on the drive allow you to define the DVD drive as a master or slave, or as CS. As a rule, avoid the use of CS. As a SCSI drive, you can place the DVD drive almost anywhere in the SCSI chain. The most critical aspect of SCSI installations is to terminate the SCSI chain properly and jumper the DVD drive with an unused SCSI ID number (usually between ID2 and ID6).

> **NOTE:** The DVD drive does not require a stand-alone MPEG-2 decoder board for basic drive operation, but the decoder is required for the playback of DVD-Video and Dolby audio.

CD-audio.   If you want to play CD audio through your sound board, you will need to connect the audio output of your DVD-ROM drive to your sound board through a thin four-wire audio cable. Make sure that the CD-ROM drive comes with a suitable connector for CD audio. Remember, unless you buy the DVD-ROM and MPEG-2 decoder board together as a multimedia kit, you may have to buy the CD audio cable separately.

> **NOTE:** Even though a sound board is not included in a DVD kit, the CD audio cable is typically included in a DVD kit.

DVD-ROM and DOS support. The immense storage capacity and enhanced multimedia capabilities of DVD make it well-positioned to replace your existing CD-ROM drive. However, there is one problem that you should be aware of: DOS support for DVD is limited and in many cases nonexistent. That is, the DVD-ROM drive will not be available under DOS because there are no real-mode drivers to operate it (even to provide backward compatibility with CDs). This was the case with the Creative Labs PC-DVD package and is something you should be sure to check before buying a new DVD kit. If you never use your CD-ROM under DOS, the issue isn't a problem. But if you still enjoy DOS games and other CD-based DOS programs, replacing the CD-ROM with a DVD drive may present a problem. In that case, you may choose to leave the existing CD-ROM in place and add the DVD-ROM as a new drive.

> **NOTE:** Both the CD-ROM and DVD-ROM support CD audio with a four-wire cable to the sound board. If you leave your existing CD-ROM in place, leave the CD audio cable attached, and play your audio CDs there rather than through the DVD drive.

MPEG-2 decoder board. One of the major advances with DVD technology is the development of high-quality video and audio playback. However, the immense volume of data required would demand several DVD discs worth of storage. In order to provide full-length feature movies on a single 4-Gbyte disc, the video and audio data must be highly *compressed* using the MPEG-2 standard. When the presentation is played, the DVD passes audio and video data to a PCI MPEG-

2 decoder board for processing. The use of hardware decoding removes a large processing burden from the system CPU. The MPEG-2 board then passes video data directly to the monitor, and audio directly to the sound board's "line input" (a pass-through is provided so that signals from your existing video board are routed through the MPEG-2 board).

> **NOTE:** Remember, the decoder board is not an interface for the DVD drive but rather a supplemental part of the complete DVD package. The decoder is not used when running programs or accessing other data from a DVD disc.

DVD manufacturers. As of this writing, the first DVD drives have started to appear. Eventually, there will be a proliferation of DVD drives to choose from. But for now, take a look at some of the early leaders:

Creative Labs   www.creaf.com

Hi-Val   www.hival.com

Diamond Multimedia   www.diamondmm.com

Other drives

Of course, there are many other possible drives that you may choose to complement the particular needs of your system. These drives are not required to make a working computer, but they can enhance the versatility of your new system. You can spend the money for other drives during your initial construction or wait and add the drives as upgrades later. Perhaps the most recognized manufacturer of "removable media" drives is Iomega (www.iomega.com). The Zip and Ditto drives are very popular.

Iomega Zip. The Zip drive has become perhaps the most popular "nonstandard" drive in production today. Zip drives offer relatively fast seek times at 29 ms, and they can sustain data rates of 300 kbytes/s across

the parallel port or 1 Mbytes/s via SCSI or IDE interfaces. Each cartridge (which resembles an ordinary
floppy disk) can hold up to 100 Mbytes, which is large
enough to hold huge illustrations, CAD layouts, and
even small multimedia presentations. When used
with an SCSI interface and a properly configured
Adaptec SCSI controller, you may even boot from the
Zip drive. Zip drives are available in both internal and
external versions.

Iomega Ditto. Tape backups are typically time-consuming and troublesome, so Iomega has developed a
tape drive that can be set up and used as quickly and
easily as possible. The result is their Ditto drive.
There are several versions of the Ditto, providing 420-
Mbyte, 800-Mbyte, and 2-Gbyte backups. According to
Iomega, the external Ditto can be installed in just 5
min, and the Ditto software makes backup operations
almost intuitive (it will even accomplish backups in
the background while you work on other things).
There are two factors to keep in mind when considering a Ditto drive. First, the Ditto 2-Gbyte drive
requires a high-performance floppy drive interface in
order to function properly. If you are using an ordinary 500-kbyte/s floppy interface, you will need to
install the Ditto Dash accelerator card. Second, the 2-
Gbyte tape is a *proprietary* tape manufactured exclusively for Iomega. The Ditto 2-Gbyte tape cartridge
uses a slightly wider tape (0.315 in) than the QIC-80
and QIC-40 minicartridges (note that the uncom-
pressed capacity for Ditto 2-Gbyte tapes is only 1
Gbyte). The 2-Gbyte tape drive can read and write to
the 2-Gbyte cartridge, but it cannot format this cartridge, so all Ditto 2-Gbyte tapes are preformatted.

Modems

There is little doubt that the Internet has become an
icon of the global information age. You can access

information, make purchases, read articles, solve technical problems, or even chat and exchange mail with anyone else on-line. If you've ever considered going on-line (or already have on-line accounts), you're going to need a modem to access the Internet, and other on-line resources such as America Online or BBS sites. Rapid advances in modem technology have resulted in dramatic increases in connection speeds, and competition has lowered the cost of modems. Intense competition between on-line service providers has also lowered the costs of going on-line. You certainly don't need a modem to get your PC up and running, but given the low cost and high performance of today's modems, it's certainly an easy thing to add to your shopping list.

Modem issues

There is not all that much to consider when selecting a modem, but those choices *are* important and can have an impact on your system setup and resources. Review the following points before making your choice.

Internal versus external.   You have the choice between internal and external modems. From a practical standpoint, both offer equivalent performance. The trade-off comes in considering your installation. Internal modems do not require a separate power supply and do not take up space outside of the PC, but they do use their own built-in Communications (COM) port (and IRQ). This means you'll need to disable or reconfigure any corresponding COM port already in the system to avoid potential hardware conflicts. By comparison, an external modem does need a separate power source and it takes up a bit of space, but you can connect it directly to any open COM port in the system. This simplifies installation a bit. Also, the external modem is mobile, and you can take it from system to system if necessary.

Modem speed. The rule with modems is "the faster the better," but faster does not always *guarantee* top-speed communication. *Both* ends of the communication link must be capable of the same top speed, or the link will be limited by the speed of the *slowest* modem. For example, if you buy a 33.6-kbyte modem and call a BBS that only has a 14.4-kbyte modem, the top speed you'll get is only 14.4 kbytes. Other factors such as poor telephone connections and incorrect drivers may also serve to reduce your communication performance. Opt for 33.6- or 56-kbyte modems if your Internet Service Provider (ISP) will support such speeds. If you really need the highest possible speeds on your desktop, contact your local telephone company to check out the costs involved with Integrated Services Digital Network (ISDN).

One other note—try to avoid the use of WinModems if at all possible. WinModem-type products compensate for highly simplified hardware by making heavy use of Windows 95 resources. Although this may not be a problem for high-powered Windows 95 platforms, older systems may be bogged down by the demands of a WinModem. Also, a WinModem will not function under DOS.

Modem drivers and software. Modems demand drivers and communication software in order to function. The new modem will come with drivers on disk, but you should also check the modem manufacturer's web site to see if there are any updates or patches available (especially if you have trouble getting the modem to work). You're also going to need communication software to run your modem. HyperTerminal—which comes with Windows 95—is a good utility for simple BBS-type connections, but a full-featured software package like SmartCom for Windows 95 can offer better control and performance. Finally, you'll need on-line access software like an Internet winsock, web browser, e-mail program, and File Transfer Program

(FTP) utility (you may choose to use Internet Explorer as well as the mail and other features that typically accompany Windows 95).

Modem manufacturers. There are a variety of modem manufacturers to choose from. Some of the more notable manufacturers are listed below:

Hayes	www.hayes.com
Motorola	www.mot.com/modems
Boca Research	www.bocaresearch.com

Input Devices

Of course, you also need to get commands and selections to the PC. This is accomplished through the use of *input devices*. As a minimum, you'll need a mouse and keyboard for your new system. If you play any sort of flight simulator or other interactive game, you should also plan on a joystick.

Mouse

Get yourself a good pointing device. It can be a mouse or a trackball (depending on your personal taste). You generally have the choice between a *serial, PS/2,* and *bus* mouse. Serial and PS/2 mice are basically the same thing—the port connectors are just a bit different. A bus mouse uses an expansion card as a mouse controller. There are no real advantages of any one type of mouse. The bus mouse frees up a serial port at the expense of a bus slot. The bus mouse controller card also demands an IRQ for proper operation, so that is one less IRQ that you will have available when adding other devices to the system. System resources are an important issue to keep in mind when choosing a mouse.

Two- or three-buttons. The choice of two- and three-button mice is really a matter of personal preference.

Most programs only recognize two buttons (left click or right click). A middle button is generally used only by specialized programs (like CAD software); otherwise, it is ignored. Unless you've got a specific use for that third mouse button, save yourself a few dollars and go with a two-button unit.

Mouse drivers. All mice require a mouse driver. If you use DOS applications, you'll need a real-mode mouse driver loaded in CONFIG.SYS or AUTOEXEC.BAT. If you use Windows 95, you'll use a protected-mode mouse driver. The drivers will accompany your mouse on floppy disk. Once you install the mouse drivers, you shouldn't need to mess with them again. If you change the mouse later, you'll need to remove the old mouse drivers before installing the new ones.

Routine maintenance. A mouse requires periodic routine maintenance to clean out the dust, debris, and hair that accumulates around the mouse ball and rollers. This typically involves removing the mouse ball and then cleaning it and the rollers. In actual practice, the process takes no longer than 5 min. Cleaning is indicated when the mouse cursor starts to "skip" or "stall" when the mouse is moved. (See App. C for more on maintenance.)

Mouse manufacturers. Pointing devices are available in a staggering array of shapes and colors from a number of different manufacturers. You can check some of the more popular pointing devices below:

Logitech   www.logitech.com
Microsoft   www.microsoft.com

Keyboard

Obviously you'll need a keyboard. There are about as many different sizes, shapes, and features for a keyboard as there are for a mouse. But there some key

points to consider. First, make sure that the keyboard
connector is compatible with the keyboard connector
on the motherboard. Today, most keyboards use the
small PS/2-type barrel connector. This is just fine.

Comfort and ergonomics. Try the keyboard if you can
to make sure that the keys *feel* comfortable. You may
also care to try an ergonomic keyboard, which is typically a bit easier on the hands and wrists. This may
seem like a trivial matter now, but better ergonomics
now can prevent persistent wrist pain later.

QWERTY versus Dvorak. You generally have two keyboard styles to choose from: QWERTY and Dvorak.
The QWERTY style is the conventional typewriter key
layout. This has been the standard typewriter layout
for 125 years, so you will have no trouble finding
QWERTY keyboards. Dvorak keyboards use a more
efficient placement of keys, which results in less fin-
ger and hand movement. This reduces hand strain
(and makes typing a bit faster). Dvorak keyboards are
harder to find, but it is possible to convert your
QWERTY keyboard to Dvorak under Windows 95.

Keyboard manufacturers. Keyboards have evolved
beyond simple typing. Many new keyboards incorporate such features as page scanners, multimedia
speakers, phone functions, integrated trackballs, and
finger-operated pointing devices. Take a look at some
of the better-known keyboard makers below:

Cirque   www.glidepoint.com
Keytronic   www.keytronic.com
NMB Technologies   www.nmbtech.com

Joystick

Joysticks are not required for the construction of your
new PC, but if you plan to do any serious flight simu-
lation or other interactive 3-D gaming, a joystick is an

absolute necessity. By themselves, joysticks are fairly
simple devices—really little more than a couple of
potentiometers, a few buttons, and a couple of springs.
But when used for PC games, the joystick adds a level
of control that is simply impossible to achieve with
any other input device.

Game ports. All joysticks require a 15-pin game port
in order to function. Most sound and I/O boards incorporate a game port already, so obtaining a game port
is not a problem. However, only one game port can be
active in the system at any given time. If you have
more than one game port in the PC, it is vital that you
remember to disable all but one. Otherwise, you'll find
that your joystick behaves erratically, and there is little (if any) control.

Joystick drivers and calibration. In the DOS world, joystick drivers were not required. Each individual application was required to service the joystick. Under
Windows 95, joystick drivers allow a single, uniform
joystick environment that any Windows 95 game can
use. Regardless of whether you use DOS or Windows
95, you will still have to calibrate the joystick periodically because of the way in which the game port reads
the analog signals from the joystick.

Routine maintenance. In general, joysticks require no
routine maintenance. Still, you'll find that the
exposed pivot of a joystick is a magnet for dust and
debris. You should make it a point to occasionally blow
out any accumulations of dust or dirt. If the joystick
experiences "dead areas" (where moving the stick
causes no change in the program), it could be that the
X or Y potentiometers are wearing out, and you
should consider replacing the joystick.

Joystick manufacturers. Although all joysticks perform the same essential functions, and they are now

available with a wide range of fancy features and "flightstick" shapes. If you're a serious game player, take a look at some of the offerings below:

Logitech	www.logitech.com
CH Products	www.chproducts.com
Gravis	www.gravis.com

2

Starting
the Assembly

The first section focused on the parts that actually go into the PC. You have had a chance to review the important subassemblies and become familiar with the major issues that you need to consider. Here, we'll go through the first part of the assembly process. By the end of this section, you should be able to boot your dream system from the floppy drive. Let's get started by gathering the parts and materials.

PC Builder's Checklist

If you haven't already purchased your parts, now is the time to make your shopping list. Table 2.1 lists the major subassemblies you'll need for your system, along with some helpful tips about what to look for. Remember that there are many variations on each of these parts (just consider the variety of motherboards and video boards in the marketplace today). This makes the actual selection process a bit challenging, but it gives you a great deal of versatility in finding the balance of price and performance that will suit your needs. Keep in mind that you don't need *every-*

TABLE 2.1 General List of Parts for New System Assembly

Item	Recommendation(s)
Case	ATX style, ample internal and external drive bays
Power supply	ATX style, 250+ W
Motherboard	ATX style, PCI bus, on-board EIDE/IDE ports
CPU	Pentium MMX 166+ MHz (remember a good heat sink/fan)
Main RAM	16+ Mbytes EDO (SDRAM if affordable)
Cache	512 kbyte (pipeline burst or better)
BIOS	Should support year 2000, USB, EIDE, power conservation, etc.
Video board	PCI, 3-D graphics acceleration, 4+ Mbyte video RAM, VESA BIOS, PnP
Monitor	SVGA, 15 to 17-in (or more), .28 or better
Sound board	On-board ATAPI IDE interface, PnP
Speakers	Full-range, 25-W rms or better
Drive controller*	EIDE, two channels (purchase only if not on motherboard)
SCSI controller*	Optional—may be needed for scanners or internal SCSI devices
Hard drive	4+ Gbyte (look for good warranty)
Floppy drive	1.44 MB 3.5 in
CD-ROM drive	8x very economical
DVD-ROM/ MPEG-2*	Wait until ample titles are available (buy as package)
Zip drive*	Optional, parallel port for portability
Jaz drive*	Optional, parallel port for portability
Tape drive*	Optional, parallel port for portability
Modem*	Internal, 33.6+ kbyte, PnP
Keyboard	any
Mouse	any
Joystick*	Optional—wait until needed
Game port*	Optional, usually incorporated into sound board or multi-I/O board
Operating system	Windows 95 (or "Memphis"/Windows 97 when available)
CD audio cable	Often comes with DVD or CD multimedia kits
EIDE/IDE cables	Get two; one for HDDs and one for CD
Floppy cable	May come with drive controller

*This part is optional—you may include it in the initial build or add it later as needed.

thing listed in Table 2.1. Everything marked with an asterisk is *optional*.

Tips for buying

Let's face it, PC parts are expensive—especially if you want top-of-the-line parts. This usually leads to some amount of anxiety when it comes time to part with your hard-earned money. However, there are a few useful tips to pass along that can take the pressure off your purchasing decisions:

■ *Understand return and exchange policies.*   This is usually where most folks get burned. Before you buy, make sure that you know how long you have to return or exchange a product if it doesn't work or proves to be incompatible. Try to avoid companies that will demand a restocking charge to take back merchandise, because you can lose as much as 20 percent of your money just for sending a product back.

■ *Use credit cards.*   This helps to ensure you don't get stiffed by fly-by-night vendors or shoddy products. If your product doesn't show up, or you can't get satisfaction from the vendor, your credit card company can become a real ally. Also, most progressive credit cards offer some form of warranty enhancement or extended protection that will help to protect your purchases beyond their manufacturer's warranty periods. Your credit card provider can give you all the details of such programs.

■ *Buy in person.*   This isn't always practical if you live in out-of-the-way places, or it may not be possible for all of your parts. But if you're fortunate enough to live in proximity to a computer superstore like CompUSA or Computer City, you may be able to pick up a selection of great parts for a very reasonable price. There are several advantages: You don't have to wait for shipping (and risk damage in transit), and you can also bring back defective or incompatible items and deal directly with a customer service person instead of playing telephone tag with an evasive service department.

- *Use mail order with caution.*   The rule of mail-order sales has always been caveat emptor, or let the buyer beware. There are many fine and reputable mail-order firms, but there are also many fly-by-night firms. With a little fancy advertising and a nice web site, it can be really hard to tell a good firm from a bad one (until it's too late). Always be sure to note the return and exchange policies of each vendor, and give their technical support a call and see if you can get through. Solicit the opinions of friends or colleagues for reputable vendors.

- *Use secure web sites.*   Use of the Internet as a sales medium has grown substantially over the last few years and is poised to enter a phase of unprecedented growth. However, Internet security to keep your confidential credit card and personal information safe continues to be an important topic. If you do elect to make purchases on-line, be sure that the site is secure. The ordering area will typically state this clearly, and your web browser will show a small key symbol somewhere in the active client window.

Tools and materials

One of the nice things about PC building is that you only need a few very basic tools to get the job done. A $15 Curtis tool kit from your local computer store will do the trick. You probably have these under your sink or in your toolbox already but run a quick check before getting started:

- Medium-sized regular screwdriver
- Medium-sized Phillips screwdriver

- Hex driver, ³⁄₁₆ in (often optional)

- Metal tweezers (to get at screws and washers dropped into tight spaces)

- Plastic washers (to space the motherboard away from metal standoffs on the case)

- Some small parts boxes or an empty egg carton to hold screws and other small parts

- A general-purpose voltmeter ($10 or $15 at your local Radio Shack)

Static precautions

If you've ever been jolted by a static charge, you can begin to appreciate the fact that static electricity can destroy the delicate ICs on your motherboard (and other boards). The problem is that you don't even know the item is damaged until you put it into place and it doesn't work. Proper handing and storage of your components is *very* important, and there are three items that you should have on hand before starting your assembly:

- An antistatic wrist strap

- An antistatic mat

- Some antistatic bags or boxes

The wrist strap drains static charge away from your body and clothing. This makes it safer to pick up and handle boards, SIMMs, CPUs, and so on. Even though you're using a wrist strap, you still need to take care to handle boards and ICs by their edges. The antistatic mat also acts as a wrist strap for your work area. Put it on your work area; it makes it safe to put things down while you're working. Antistatic bags and boxes allow you to store boards and ICs safely. You should keep devices in their protective packaging until you're *just* ready to install them. If you're removing an existing (but working) device, place it directly into protective packaging for storage or return. Trust me—static damage has caused a lot of grief over the years. Do yourself a favor and use good antistatic precautions.

Boot disk

Your toolbox won't be complete without a boot disk. You'll need this to initially start up your PC and prepare your hard drive for service. There are two means of creating a boot disk: automatically through an existing Windows 95 platform or manually through a DOS 6.22 platform. In either case, you're going to need access to a running PC with an operating system similar to the version you plan to install on the new PC.

Windows 95.   Windows 95 comes with an automatic start-up disk maker. If you have access to a Windows 95 system, use the following procedure to create a DOS 7.x start-up disk:

- Label a blank disk and insert it into your floppy drive.

- Click on *Start, Settings,* and *Control Panel.*

- Double-click on the *Add/Remove Programs* icon.

- Select the *Startup Disk* tab as in Fig. 2.1.

- Click on *Create Disk.*

- The utility will remind you to insert a disk and then will prepare the disk automatically. When the preparation is complete, test the disk.

The preparation process takes several minutes and will copy the following files to your disk: ATTRIB, CHKDSK, COMMAND, DEBUG, DRVSPACE.BIN, EDIT, FDISK, FORMAT, REGEDIT, SCANDISK, SYS, and UNINSTAL. All of these files are DOS 7.x-based files, so you can run them from the A: prompt.

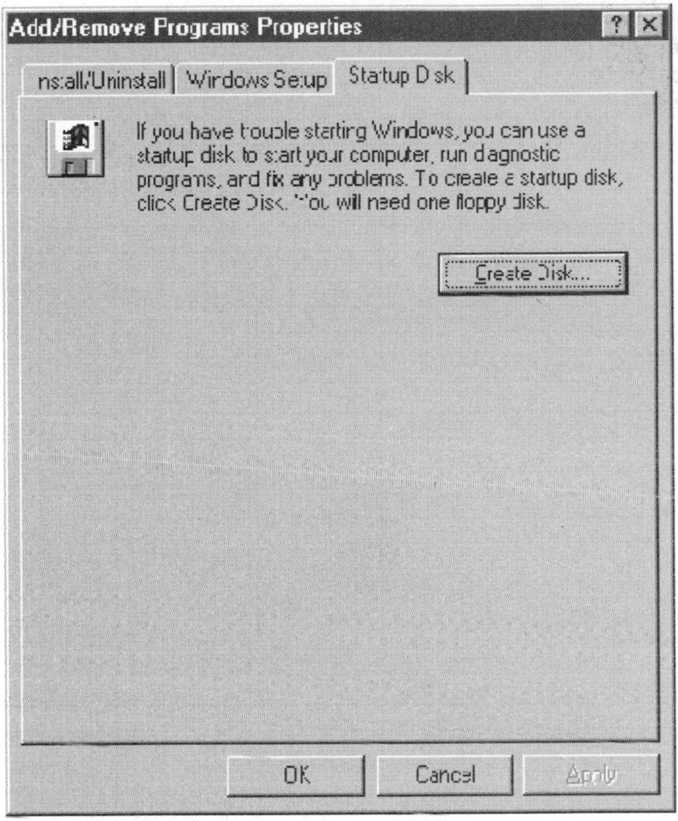

Figure 2.1 The Windows 95 start-up disk maker.

NOTE: The Windows 95 FDISK utility has been reported to have a bug that can cause problems when creating more than one partition on the same drive. Later releases of Windows 95 claim to have corrected this issue, but if you encounter problems with FDISK, use the DOS 6.22 version.

DOS 6.22. If you don't have access to a system with Windows 95 already, you'll need to make a boot disk manually using DOS 6.22 utilities. Create a bootable disk by using the SYS feature as follows:

```
C:\DOS\> SYS A:  <ENTER>
```

or use the FORMAT command to make a bootable disk:

```
C:\DOS\> FORMAT A: /S  <ENTER>
```

Once the disk is bootable, copy the following DOS utilities (usually from the DOS directory): FDISK, FORMAT, SYS, MEM, DEFRAG, SCANDISK, EDIT, HIMEM, EMM386, and EDIT. You may not need all of these utilities, but it can be handy to have them on hand.

Work area

Whether you are building a new system or troubleshooting your existing PC, you'll need to select a good work area. In general, select a heated, dry area that offers *ample* building space and lighting. You should (if possible) select a quiet, low-traffic area free of pets, spouses, children, and other minor distractions. I also suggest that you put down ample paper (such as old newspaper) to protect your work area. Otherwise, you're liable to drop a screwdriver and ding the kitchen table. Finally, if you do use an anti-static mat as advised, do *not* assemble anything on top of the mat. The mat is strictly for use as a temporary "static safe" holding area for delicate electronics.

Electrical safety

From a practical standpoint, it is virtually impossible to injure yourself with electricity while building a PC. The power supply is totally enclosed, and the connectors are designed to minimize the chances of accidental contact. However, I still must remind you that the AC coming from your wall outlet is dangerous, and a shock hazard may exist as long as the PC cover is removed. For total safety, *keep the PC unplugged and turned off whenever you're working on it*. If you must fire it up for a test, keep your hands out of the system until you have turned off and unplugged the power supply again. I should also advise you to have handy a fire extinguisher that is capable of dealing with electrical-type fires.

Case and Power Supply Assembly

Let's start by assembling your case and installing the power supply. If you already have a preassembled case and installed power supply, feel free to skip this section (although you may still want to read it for reference).

Step 1: Assemble the case

Most cases are preassembled— this simplifies things quite a bit. If you *must* assemble a case on your own, be sure to follow all of the manufacturer's instructions that accompany the case. Contrary to popular belief, it's not OK to have extra parts when you're done. When complete, the case should be sturdy and rigid. If it wiggles like a bowl of Jell-O, go back and check your work now.

> **NOTE:** Do not proceed with the assembly until your case is assembled correctly and mechanically sound.

Edges and points.   Whether you assemble your own case or not, you will need to watch out for sharp edges and burrs in the metal—especially in the drive bays and metal housing, which you'll be working with most closely. Low-end manufacturers often save costs by ignoring that tedious, time-consuming finish work (such as dulling sharp edges and removing burrs). This can result in cuts and abrasions as you handle the case. As a rule, use caution when handling any of the metal enclosures. It may help to use a set of light work gloves when assembling the case.

Fans and filters.   Your case may also include fans and filters. Fans are used to vent heated air from the case area. Often one fan blows air in, and another fan blows air out. In tower cases, the intake fan is located in the lower front, and the exhaust fan is located in the upper rear. Desktop cases may only use a single exhaust fan located in the rear. Intake filters are sometimes used with good-quality cases to trap the dust and other airborne debris that normally enters the enclosure. Because dust is an electrical conductor and thermal insulator, minimizing dust with a filter is certainly a worthwhile precaution. You should periodically clean fan blades and filters to remove any accumulations of dust and debris.

Notes on upgrading a case.   If you are planning to replace your existing case (typically as part of a broader upgrade strategy), you will need to *completely* disassemble your system and then reassemble it in the new case—just as if you were assembling a new PC from scratch. Follow Secs. 2 and 3 for a full assembly order. When removing parts, you should make it a point to mark cables with masking tape and indelible markers. This way, you can quickly identify where each item goes during reassembly (especially those pesky little wires that connect to the front panel).

Consider upgrading the case and power supply together and leaving the old case and power supply mated as a single assembly. This strategy costs a bit more because it requires you to purchase a new power supply for the new case, but it is much easier to build up a new system later in the old case or even sell off the old case if there is already a working power supply installed.

Step 2: Install the power supply

Once the case is built, it's time to install the power supply. If the power supply is already incorporated into the case, you're in luck. Otherwise, you'll need to mount the power supply in the case. Make sure that the AC line cord connection, the fuse (or circuit breaker) access, the AC voltage (120/220 Vac) selector switch, and the power on/off switch are all readily accessible. Also check to see that the power supply mounting holes line up with the holes in the case (ideally, you already did that before you bought the power supply).

> NOTE: Be sure to use the right screws when bolting the power supply into place. If the screws are too long, they may damage wiring or crack a circuit board in the power supply.

Presetting the power supply.   Before you go any farther, let's preconfigure your power supply and make sure that it is receiving power properly:

- Check to make sure that the AC voltage selector switch (120/220 Vac) is set in the proper position. In the domestic United States, the switch should be set to 120 Vac. In Europe, the switch is typically set to 220 Vac.

- Check the power switch and see that it is turned *off*.

- Connect the AC line cord to the power supply and then plug it into an AC outlet.

- Turn the power supply on. The cooling fan should start and run quietly. If it doesn't, recheck the AC voltage selector and AC line cord installation. If problems persist, try a new power supply.

- Once you confirm that the power supply fan is running, turn off the power supply and unplug it from the AC outlet.

Notes on upgrading a power supply. Power supply
upgrades are a breeze—assuming that the new power
supply fits and aligns with the mounting holes.
Simply unplug the AC line cord, unplug the motherboard power connectors, unplug the drive power connectors, and then unbolt and remove the power supply
unit. Set the power supply aside. Set the new power
supply into place and secure it carefully (be sure to
use any lock washers or other mounting hardware).
Plug in the motherboard power connectors and then
plug in the drive power cables. Finally, you can install
the AC line cord and power the system up.

Assembling the Main Board

Now that the case and power supply are assembled,
you'll need to install the motherboard, as well as the
motherboard support components such as the CPU,
RAM, and cache.

Step 3A: Motherboard
installation

At this point, your case is ready to accept the motherboard and supplemental devices such as the CPU,
RAM, and cache. Remember to use good static precautions to prevent accidental damage to the motherboard's sensitive electronics. Keep the motherboard in
its protective antistatic packaging until you are *just*
ready to bolt it into place. The actual physical installation is quite straightforward, but subsequent sections will offer additional installation details:

1. Place small nonconductive plastic washers on each
   of the metal standoffs as illustrated in Fig. 2.2.
   This prevents the standoffs from shorting out the
   motherboard wiring and causing system problems.
   Remember that your washers must be as thin as
   possible. Otherwise, your expansion bus slots will

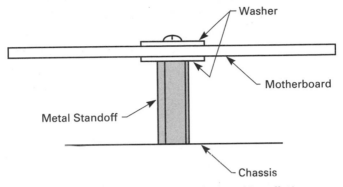

Figure 2.2 Placing washers during motherboard installation.

sit a bit too high, and you won't be able to bolt expansion boards to the chassis securely.

2. Seat the motherboard into place and see that each mounting hole lines up with the standoffs on your case (ideally, you did that before buying the motherboard). Also see that all of those washers are still in place.

3. Place some more small nonconductive plastic washers on top of each mounting hole. This prevents the metal head of each screw from shorting out the motherboard wiring on the top of the motherboard and causing system problems.

4. Make sure that the motherboard's expansion slots are aligned correctly with the openings in the back of the case. Also make sure that all ports (i.e., video ports, parallel ports, and so on) are readily accessible from the back of the case.

5. Install all of the mounting screws and secure the motherboard into place. Do not use excessive force when tightening the screws—just snug them down.

6. Install the motherboard power connector(s). Check out the motherboard's documentation to see exactly which connector goes where. For Baby AT-type power supplies, you'll have two 6-pin Molex con-

nectors (the black wires of both motherboard power supply connectors go together). For ATX-type power supplies, there is a single 20-pin connector. Be sure to orient the connector properly.

7. Install the wires from the front case such as for the turbo Light Emitting Diode (LED), the Reset button, and so on (more details are provided below).

8. Install the CPU, RAM, and cache (more details are provided below).

> **NOTE:** Take great care that no part of the motherboard is bent (not even a little) or shorted against any part of the case. If it is, you'll need to reseat the motherboard in order to correct the problem.

Step 3B: Case wiring

Chances are that your case will have several features such as a power LED, a hard drive activity LED, and a Reset button (just to name a few). Other cases may also have a key switch, a turbo switch, and turbo LED. Each of these switches and LEDs are wired to short, two- or three-wire cables (usually harnessed near the case's front panel). Once the motherboard is mounted properly, you'll need to connect those wires to their appropriate places on the motherboard, and this is usually where new PC builders start getting nervous. Get out your motherboard documentation and locate the case connectors. Figure 2.3 illustrates the case connections for a typical motherboard. Simply route each cable from the case to its corresponding motherboard connection. Here is a rundown of the most common cables:

- Power LED—usually to a two-pin header on the motherboard
- Key switch—usually to a two- or three-pin header on the motherboard

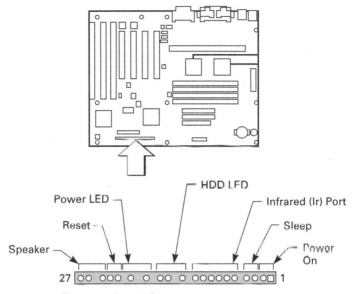

Figure 2.3 Diagram of typical case connectors.

- Hard Disk Drive (HDD) LED —to the hard drive (leave it loose for now)

- Reset switch—usually to a two-pin header on the motherboard

- Turbo switch—usually to a two- or three-pin header on the motherboard

- Turbo LED—to a two-pin header on the mother-board

Keep in mind that not all systems will sport *all* of these features. The case may offer features that the motherboard doesn't use (and vice versa). You will need to review the motherboard manual for your specific motherboard to learn where each connection is located and which ones perform what role. When you're actually installing the case wiring, there are two issues to keep in mind:

1. Switches are nonpolarized devices, so it really doesn't matter if you reverse the connector's orientation or not. If you reverse a three-pin cable and find the related feature to be working backward (like a keyboard being locked in the unlocked position and unlocked in the locked position), simply reverse the connector.

2. LEDs *are* polarized devices and can only be installed one way. However, you cannot damage the LED by reversing it—it just won't light up. If the LED does not light up, just reverse the connector.

Step 3C: CPU installation

Now it's time to install the CPU. You'll need to configure the motherboard to accommodate the CPU correctly by setting the CPU Type/Voltage jumper, the Clock Speed jumper, and the Multiplier jumper and then perform the physical CPU installation. If the CPU is already installed and configured on the motherboard, feel free to skip this section—although you may find this to be a good reference.

CPU type/voltage jumper.   Older OverDrive-compatible motherboards used CPU-type jumpers to identify the specific CPU installed in the socket. This allowed the BIOS to identify the CPU and make any necessary firmware changes to drive the system properly. Today, the BIOS can essentially autoidentify a CPU, and the CPU-type jumpers are now used to trim CPU operating voltages.

Modern microprocessors use slightly different voltage levels from manufacturer to manufacturer. You will have to identify the proper CPU type being installed so that the voltage regulator circuit on the motherboard can set the proper operating voltage. If the CPU voltage is set too low, you risk data errors and system lockups. If the voltage is set too high, the CPU

will run unusually hot, and you risk burning out the
CPU (an expensive proposition). Take extra care to set
the right CPU voltage levels as illustrated in Table 2.2.
If your motherboard does not have an on-board voltage
regulator, you will need to purchase a regulator module along with your CPU. A *Voltage Regulator Module*
(VRM) looks like a big CPU socket and fits between
the CPU and the motherboard's CPU socket.

Clock speed and multiplier jumpers. Before installing
your CPU, you'll also need to configure the motherboard's bus speed and multiplier. *Bus speed* indicates
the clock rate (in megahertz, or MHz) that is driving
the CPU. The *multiplier* indicates how much the CPU
is boosting the bus speed to achieve its rated operating frequency. Locate the clock speed and multiplier
jumpers on your motherboard now, and set them
according to Table 2.3. Note that the exact number of
clock and multiplier jumpers will vary depending on
the range of frequencies available and the number of
CPU models your motherboard will support.

CPU heat sink/fan. Now examine the CPU itself
(*remember to use all antistatic precautions*). All CPUs
generate heat as they consume power, and fast CPUs
(133+ MHz) can run blazing hot. You must keep the
CPU cool to ensure its proper operation and long, reliable life. Invest in a heat sink/fan that is sized *properly* for your CPU. The heat sink draws heat away from

**TABLE 2.2 CPU Type and Voltage Selections for a Typical
Pentium Motherboard**

CPU type	Typical voltage(s) (V)
Pentium Classic Sxx-type CPU or Cyrix/IBM 6x86	3.30 (STD)
Pentium Classic Vxx-type CPU or Cyrix/IBM 6x86	3.53 (VRE)
Pentium MMX CPU or Cyrix/IBM 6x86L and M2	2.8/3.3
AMD K6 (PR2-166 and PR2-200)	2.9/3.3
AMD K6 (PR2-233)	3.2/3.3

TABLE 2.3 Index of Clock Speed and Multiplier Settings

CPU speed (MHz)	Bus speed (MHz)	Multiplier
Intel Pentium/MMX CPUs		
75	50	1.5
90	60	1.5
100	66	1.5
120	60	2.0
133	66	2.0
150	60	2.5
166	66	2.5
180	60	3.0
200	66	3.0
233	66	3.5
AMD CPUs		
AMD-K5-PR75 75	50	1.5
AMD-K5-PR90 90	60	1.5
AMD-K5-PR100 100	66	1.5
AMD-K5-PR120 90	60	1.5
AMD-K5-PR133 133	66	2.0
AMD-K5-PR166 166	66	2.5
AMD-K6-PR166 166	66	2.5
AMD-K6-PR200 200	66	3.0
AMD-K6-PR233 233	66	3.5
Cyrix CPUs		
Cyrix PR150+ 120	60	2.0
Cyrix PR166+ 133	66	2.0

the CPU, and the built-in fan makes the cooling process much more efficient. Improperly cooled CPUs can overheat, resulting in random system crashes and lockups.

In many cases, you can purchase a heat sink fan already attached to the CPU. If you must install one yourself (i.e., if you replace a failed heat sink/fan), spread a thin layer of *thermal grease* over the CPU. Thermal grease is a thick, white substance with a somewhat acrid smell (you may initially mistake it for adhesive, but it is *not* an adhesive). The grease greatly aids the transfer of heat from the CPU to the heat sink. The heat sink/fan assembly then usually clips onto the CPU. Sometimes, the heat sink/fan clips to the CPU socket, so you'll have to insert the CPU in the socket before installing the cooling unit. Remember that the heat sink/fan *must* fit securely. If the heat sink/fan is loose or does not clip on securely, *bring it back*—your vendor may have given you the wrong one.

> **NOTE:** Heat sink/fans all do the exact same job, but do yourself a favor and invest in a good-quality unit (something with a ball bearing fan assembly). Cheap fans make lots of noise and can fail quickly—leaving your CPU without proper cooling.

> **NOTE:** Thermal grease *will* easily stain fabrics, so be sure to use it sparingly, keep the grease tube capped, and be careful when you wipe off the residue.

The fan itself is powered by one of those four-pin drive power cables, so connect the fan power now. If you do not have enough power cables to operate the heat sink/fan, as well as the other drives you plan to add, use a Y-splitter cable if necessary to split one power cable into two. Use one end for the heat sink/fan, and use the other end to power your floppy drive.

> **NOTE:** Do *not* split power from a hard drive.

CPU alignment.   Next, you need to install the CPU in its socket. Most motherboards use a Zero Insertion Force (ZIF) socket, which allows you to insert the CPU easily and then lock it into place. The most important consideration here is to make sure that the CPU is inserted in the proper orientation. Align pin 1 of the CPU with pin 1 on the socket, ease the CPU gently into the socket until it sits flush, and then close the locking lever to secure the CPU into place. Refer to the motherboard's particular documentation to determine exactly where pin 1 on the CPU should go. If you're upgrading an existing CPU, make note of the original CPU's alignment before removing it.

> **NOTE:** CPU alignment is a serious matter. If the CPU is installed in the wrong orientation, power and ground will be applied to the wrong CPU pins. This may damage and ruin the CPU.

CPU sockets.   If you work with motherboards to any extent, you're going to encounter terms like *Socket 7* or other socket designations. Over the years, a whole range of socket designs have evolved to accommodate different CPUs. Today, Socket 7 is the traditional socket for virtually all Pentium and Pentium MMX-type CPUs, so you will see motherboards marked "Socket 7 compatible." Table 2.4 shows you a comparison of socket types. Remember that all sockets use ZIF technology to allow easy insertion and removal of the CPU. Whenever installing a new CPU, be sure that the tension lever is locked down and secure. If the lever is not secure, it can pop up and relieve tension from the CPU. This can cause erratic system operation and crashes.

Step 3D: RAM installation

You'll need to install RAM on the motherboard. Some motherboards incorporate 2 to 4 Mbytes of RAM soldered right to the motherboard and then provide

TABLE 2.4 **Compatibility Details for Major Sockets**

Socket	Pins	Volts	CPU
Socket 1	169	5	486 SX
			486 DX
Socket 2	238	5	486 SX
			486 DX
			486 DX2
Socket 3	237	3/5	486 SX
			486 DX
			486 DX2
			486 DX4
Socket 4	273	5	60/66-MHz Pentium
Socket 5	320	3	75/90/100-MHz Pentium
Socket 6	235	3	486 DX4
Socket 7	321	2.5/3.3	75/90/100-MHz Pentium
Socket 8	387	2.5	Pentium Pro
Slot 1	242	N/A	Pentium II

space for 32 Mbytes or more in the form of 30- or 72-pin SIMMs. Most motherboards today are eliminating hard soldered RAM entirely and instead allow you to add 128 Mbyte or more of RAM in terms of SIMMs or 168-pin DIMMs. Eliminating on-board RAM from the motherboard is preferred because it is much easier to replace a defective SIMM or DIMM if memory fails. Otherwise, you'd need to replace the entire motherboard.

Clipping the SIMMs and DIMMs in place. Installing a memory device is quick and easy. They are all polarized devices with a physical "key" notched into one end. The SIMM will only fit into its slot *one way*. Sit the SIMM completely into its slot and then ease it back into its holder until the SIMM clips into place. You must do this gently because you can easily snap the clips of the SIMM holder. If you wish to remove a SIMM for upgrade, you must gently ease back the clips at both ends of the SIMM, which will free the SIMM. Then just tilt the SIMM forward and remove it from the socket.

NOTE: If you *do* snap a clip off a SIMM holder, you can usually still hold the SIMM in place by using an elastic band around the SIMM and holder. Do *not* use tape because tape eventually becomes gummy (loosing its adhesive qualities).

DIMM installation is very similar to SIMM installation. Hold the DIMM so that its notched edge is aligned with the notch on the DIMM socket. If notched edges do not match, you are probably using the incorrect type of DIMM (i.e., using a buffered DIMM in an unbuffered socket or vice versa). Insert the DIMM at a 90 degree angle (straight down) and then gently push the DIMM straight down until it locks into place past its release tabs. To remove a DIMM later, push the release tabs away and pull the DIMM straight out.

NOTE: Remember that SIMMs and DIMMs are *very* static sensitive, so always use static precautions when handling these memory devices. Keep SIMMs and DIMMs in their antistatic packaging until you're *just* ready to install them. When removing SIMMs or DIMMs, place them *directly* into antistatic bags.

Another note to keep in mind when installing or upgrading SIMMs and DIMMs is to match the metals on the SIMM or DIMM contacts with the contact metal on your holders. For example, many SIMM holders use tin-plated contacts. As a result, you should choose SIMMs with tin plated contacts. If the SIMM holder has gold-plated contacts, you should choose SIMMs with gold-plated contacts. Mixing contact metals can cause contact corrosion and result in memory errors.

Filling a bank.   When adding SIMMs, you must *always* add enough SIMMs to fill an entire bank (you learned about the concept of banks briefly in the first chapter). For example, a Pentium CPU is a 64-bit (8-byte) CPU, so you need *two* 72-pin (4-byte) SIMMs or *one* 168-pin

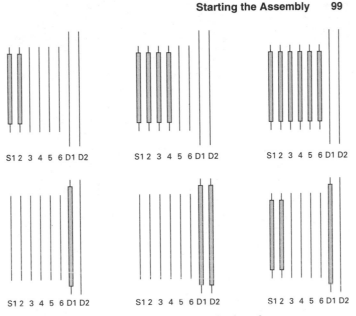

Figure 2.4 Filling memory banks on a motherboard.

(8-byte) DIMM to fill one Pentium memory bank. Figure 2.4 illustrates several bank-filling strategies for a typical motherboard. When filling banks, you should observe the following rules:

- Memory must be contiguous, so start by filling bank 0 and then fill subsequent banks in order (i.e., bank 1, bank 2, and so on).

- When filling a bank, all of the SIMMs within any given bank must be the same size (i.e., 4 MB×32), speed (i.e., 60 ns), type (i.e., EDO or SDRAM), and parity (nonparity or parity).

- If you are using slower and faster SIMMs together in the same system, place the slower SIMMs in the first bank (i.e., bank 0) and then place the faster SIMMs in subsequent banks.

SIMM combinations. Today's motherboards support huge amounts of RAM—up to 512 Mbytes of RAM in some cases. Although it is unlikely that you will use nearly that much RAM, you are going to have to decide how much RAM to add and which bank to add it in. For example, you may have two 2Mx32 SIMMs (16 Mbyte total) in the first bank but add two 1Mx32 SIMMs (8 Mbyte total) to the second bank for a total of 24 Mbytes. On the other hand, you may add two 4Mx32 SIMMS (32 Mbytes total) to the second bank for a total of 48 Mbytes. In other words, you do not *have* to add memory in consistent increments. However, not all motherboards allow *all* combinations of SIMM sizes in every bank (or all combinations of SIMMs and DIMMs), so before you run out and buy memory to fill that second bank, make sure to check your motherboard's documentation to find which memory combinations are allowed (or at least find any that are specifically prohibited). Table 2.5 lists possible memory combinations for a typical Pentium motherboard. This motherboard has six 72-pin SIMM slots (three banks) plus two 168-pin DIMM slots (two banks). Choose the total amount of RAM needed for your system from the left column and then find the recommended SIMM/DIMM combinations.

> **NOTE:** Table 2.5 does not include "mixed" SIMM and DIMM configurations. Refer to your motherboard's documentation for such detailed instructions.

Mixing SIMM types. In the first section, you learned about several different types of RAM (i.e., DRAM, EDO, FPM, and so on). These RAM types are all based on basic DRAM and are optimized in an effort to increase memory performance. This has a tremendous impact on system performance because the CPU must usually wait for the memory to catch up. If the memory is faster, the CPU will "waste" less time, and the overall system performance improves. Mixing these types of memory is sometimes problematic:

TABLE 2.5 Memory Combinations for a Typical Motherboard

Memory size (Mbytes)	SIMM 1	SIMM 2	SIMM 3	SIMM 4	SIMM 5	SIMM 6	DIMM 1	DIMM 2
8	1Mx32	1Mx32						
8							1Mx64	
16	2Mx32	2Mx32						
16	1Mx32	1Mx32	1Mx32	1Mx32				
16							2Mx64	
16							1Mx64	1Mx64
24	1Mx32	1Mx32	2Mx32	2Mx32				
24	1Mx32	1Mx32	1Mx32	1Mx32	1Mx32	1Mx32		
24							1Mx64	2Mx64
32	4Mx32	4Mx32						
32	2Mx32	2Mx32	2Mx32	2Mx32				
32	1Mx32	1Mx32	1Mx32	1Mx32	2Mx32	2Mx32		
32							4Mx64	
32							2Mx64	2Mx64
40	1Mx32	1Mx32	4Mx32	4Mx32				
40							1Mx64	4Mx64
48	2Mx32	2Mx32	4Mx32	4Mx32				
48	1Mx32	1Mx32	1Mx32	1Mx32	4Mx32	4Mx32		
48	2Mx32	2Mx32	2Mx32	2Mx32	2Mx32	2Mx32		
48							2Mx64	4Mx64
64	8Mx32	8Mx32						

TABLE 2.5 Memory Combinations for a Typical Motherboard (Continued)

Memory size (Mbytes)	SIMM 1	SIMM 2	SIMM 3	SIMM 4	SIMM 5	SIMM 6	DIMM 1	DIMM 2
64	4Mx32	4Mx32	4Mx32	4Mx32				
64	2Mx32	2Mx32	2Mx32	2Mx32	4Mx32	4Mx32		
64							8Mx64	
64							4Mx64	4Mx64
72	1Mx32	1Mx32	8Mx32	8Mx32				
72							1Mx64	8Mx64
80	2Mx32	2Mx32	8Mx32	8Mx32				
80	1Mx32	1Mx32	1Mx32	1Mx32	8Mx32	8Mx32		
80							2Mx64	8Mx64
96	4Mx32	4Mx32	8Mx32	8Mx32				
96	2Mx32	2Mx32	2Mx32	2Mx32	8Mx32	8Mx32		
96	4Mx32	4Mx32	4Mx32	4Mx32	4Mx32	4Mx32		
96							4Mx64	8Mx64
128	16Mx32	16Mx32						
128	8Mx32	8Mx32	8Mx32	8Mx32				
128	4Mx32	4Mx32	4Mx32	4Mx32	8Mx32	8Mx32		
128							8Mx64	8Mx64
136	1Mx32	1Mx32	16Mx32	16Mx32				
144	2Mx32	2Mx32	16Mx32	16Mx32				
144	1Mx32	1Mx32	1Mx32	1Mx32	16Mx32	16Mx32		
160	4Mx32	4Mx32	16Mx32	16Mx32				

160	2Mx32	2Mx32	2Mx32	2Mx32			
192	8Mx32	8Mx32	16Mx32	16Mx32	16Mx32	16Mx32	
192	4Mx32	4Mx32	4Mx32	4Mx32	8Mx32	8Mx32	
192	8Mx32	8Mx32	8Mx32	8Лx32			
256	32Mx32	32Mx32					
256	16Mx32	16Mx32	16Mx32	16Mx32	16Mx32	16Mx32	
256	8Mx32	8Mx32	8Mx32	8Mx32	8Mx32	8Mx32	
256						16Mx64	16Mx64

- Generally speaking, you can use enhanced memory on motherboards that do not support it, and you simply will not enjoy the performance advantage that the memory offers. Conversely, you can usually use ordinary DRAM in motherboards that accept enhanced memory, but you also will not enjoy any performance advantages.

- The time you can run into trouble is when mixing types within the same bank or system. It may be possible to support several different types of RAM in the same system, but as a rule, if you choose to use EDO memory, all the memory should be EDO. If you add a bank of FPM memory, you may have problems.

Memory parity.   Parity—simply stated—is a byte-level form of error checking that allows the motherboard to catch single-bit errors when reading from memory. A parity bit is added to every byte in RAM (so a 2Mx32 SIMM would have 4 bytes only with no parity, and a 2Mx36 SIMM would have 4 extra bits for parity). The motherboard calculates a parity bit for the byte read and then compares that bit against the parity bit read from memory. If the parity bits match, the byte is assumed good, and the system moves along. If not, an error is flagged and the system halts. In truth, parity checking is an inefficient and limited form of error checking, and it cannot correct errors. Industry opponents claim that the frequency of memory errors is so small that the expense of the extra 4 bits can be saved to reduce the cost of RAM even further. On the other hand, ignoring error checking can have catastrophic consequences on your system if left unchecked, and advanced forms of memory error checking and correction (such as ECC) are not yet in broad use. My feeling is that it is well worth the extra money to buy and use parity RAM to protect your system from random bit errors and memory failures.

NOTE: If you choose to use parity checking, all the RAM in your system *must* be parity RAM (×M×36). If you choose to use *any* nonparity RAM (×M×32), parity checking on your motherboard must be turned *off* (usually through the CMOS Setup).

Step 3E: Cache RAM installation

Cache is used as a performance enhancement that stores frequently used information in very fast SRAM (on the order of 10 to 15 ns). The CPU can access cache without using wait states, so the resulting performance is vastly improved. Motherboards typically use between 128 and 512 kbytes of cache, with most now using 512 kbytes. Unlike SIMMs, which are available in a wide variety of sizes and speeds, cache is typically provided in one of three forms depending on the design of your selected motherboard: It is soldered on-board (and unchangable), it is provided in the form of DIP ICs that must be plugged into the motherboard individually, or it is provided on COAST modules (which resemble SIMMs and are much easier to install).

NOTE: In many cases, you do not have to actually install cache. It typically comes preinstalled when you purchase the motherboard. Still, you should be familiar with the configuration and upgrade issues if you need to work with cache RAM.

Choosing your cache.   Generally, stepping from 128 to 256 kbytes yields a dramatic improvement. Stepping from 256 to 512 kbytes offers some additional improvement but not nearly as much. As a rule, make sure that your motherboard has at least 256 kbytes of cache. If you can afford the extra 256 kbytes, and optimum performance is your goal, go ahead and add the other 256 kbytes to bring your total to 512 kbytes. Some current motherboards will support up to 1

Mbyte of cache, although this is only beneficial if you are using a huge amount of RAM (i.e., 64 Mbytes or more) in your system.

Installing and upgrading cache RAM.   Cache is added as traditional DIP ICs that are usually socket mounted in a corner of the motherboard—often near the SIMMs or CPU. You install cache by simply plugging new cache RAM ICs into their respective sockets. Use extreme caution with DIP ICs. You can easily bend their pins during insertion. This ruins the IC. You also must be sure that the IC is aligned properly with pin 1 on the socket. Reversing the IC will damage it (and probably prevent the PC from booting). Once cache is installed, you may need to change a motherboard jumper to specify the new amount of cache available. On some motherboards, that change can be made in the CMOS Setup once power is restored to the system.

More recently, COAST modules have become popular. COAST modules resemble SIMMs and are plugged into a specially designed socket on the motherboard. Your choice of cache will depend on the motherboard. If the motherboard provides DIP sockets for cache, you will need DIP ICs. If the motherboard provides a COAST socket, you will need a COAST module.

Upgrading your cache requires direct replacement rather than additional memory. You will need to remove the existing DIP ICs (or COAST module) and install the new, larger DIP ICs (or COAST module). You will then need to identify the extra cache through a motherboard jumper or a CMOS Setup entry.

Step 3F: CMOS battery installation

Your system's setup parameters are stored in a small quantity of low-power RAM called CMOS RAM. Because RAM loses its contents when power is removed, power is required to maintain your CMOS

settings. Because CMOS RAM requires only a very
small amount of power, a battery is used to maintain
the contents of this RAM while main system power is
off. In fact, *so* little power is used that a typical CMOS
backup battery can last for years. If you don't already
have a battery on the motherboard, you will need to
add one. A motherboard will typically include a battery, but it will not be installed. CMOS backup batteries can take several different forms:

- *Coin cells.*   This is the classic backup battery. It is
  small, inexpensive, and can be installed quickly
  and easily on the motherboard. Your only real concern is to watch out for the cell's polarity. It should
  not damage anything if you reverse the battery, but
  it will not maintain your CMOS RAM when power
  is turned off.

- *Battery packs.*   Most motherboards supplement
  the on-board battery by providing a four-pin connector for an *external* battery pack. The advantage
  of a battery pack is that the batteries often last
  much longer than other battery types and may be
  your only alternative if your motherboard uses a
  proprietary battery that is no longer in production.
  The pack itself is attached to the case with a piece
  of Velcro and is connected to the motherboard by a
  short cable. You may need to switch a jumper on
  the motherboard to choose between an on-board
  battery and a battery pack.

- *Integrated batteries.*   Some motherboards use specialized CMOS RAM Real Time Clock (RTC)
  devices that actually integrate the battery into the
  device (Dallas Semiconductor is renowned for this
  tactic). When you examine the motherboard, you
  won't find a battery anywhere, so look for a device
  marked "Dallas" or "RTC." The CMOS RAM/RTC
  unit is mounted on a socket so that it can be
  replaced when the battery wears out.

- *Barrel batteries.*   Finally, many motherboards use a battery that looks like a little blue or green barrel and is soldered into the motherboard. You don't need to install such a battery, but you should recognize it when you see it. These batteries provide a good working life but cannot be replaced (without the hazardous process of desoldering the original battery and then soldering in a new one). However, you can always use a battery pack if the barrel battery fails.

Motherboard problems and troubleshooting

In general, motherboard problems will have serious consequences on the operation of your system (if the system even starts). But this portion of the section is designed to familiarize you with the two tools you have available for motherboard troubleshooting: beep codes and POST codes.

Beep codes.   Beep codes are a series of speaker beeps that are generated if a problem is detected *before* the video system is initialized. Each BIOS version uses its own set of beep codes (which is typically included in your motherboard's documentation), so by matching the beep code to your particular BIOS, you can determine the exact problem. For example, Table 2.6 below shows the beep codes for a recent Phoenix BIOS. Suppose your system uses a Phoenix BIOS, and you hear a beep sequence of 1-1-3-3. This means the CPU registers couldn't be initialized and may suggest a fault in the CPU.

POST codes.   As you saw in Sec. 1, the BIOS performs a series of tests on the hardware each time your system is powered up. Each test generates a single-byte (8-bit) hexadecimal code that is sent to I/O port 80h in your PC (some PC designs use different port addresses). If

TABLE 2.6 Beep and POST Codes for the Phoenix 4.0 BIOS

Beep	POST	Meaning
1-1-1-3	02	Verify real-mode operation
1-1-2-1	04	Get the CPU type
1-1-2-3	06	Initialize system hardware
1-1-3-1	08	Initialize chipset registers with POST values
1-1-3-2	09	Set POST flag
1-1-3-3	0A	Initialize CPU registers
1-1-4-1	0C	Initialize cache to initial POST values
1-1-4-3	0E	Initialize I/O
1-2-1-1	10	Initialize Power Management
1-2-1-2	11	Load alternate registers with POST values
1-2-1-3	12	Jump to UserPatch0
1-2-2-1	14	Initialize keyboard controller
1-2-2-3	16	BIOS ROM checksum
1-2-3-1	18	8254 timer initialization
1-2-3-3	1A	8237 DMA controller initialization
1-2-4-1	1C	Reset Programmable Interrupt Controller
1-3-1-1	20	Test DRAM refresh
1-3-1-3	22	Test 8742 keyboard controller
1-3-2-1	24	Set ES segment to register to 4 GB
1-3-3-1	28	Autosize DRAM
1-3-3-3	2A	Clear 512K base RAM
1-3-4-1	2C	Test 512K base address lines
1-3-4-3	2E	Test 512K base memory
1-4-1-3	32	Test CPU bus-clock frequency
1-4-2-4	37	Reinitialize the motherboard chipset
1-4-3-1	38	Shadow system BIOS ROM
1-4-3-2	39	Reinitialize the cache
1-4-3-3	3A	Autosize cache
1-4-4-1	3C	Configure advanced chipset registers
1-4-4-2	3D	Load alternate registers with CMOS values
2-1-1-1	40	Set initial CPU speed
2-1-1-3	42	Initialize interrupt vectors
2-1-2-1	44	Initialize BIOS interrupts
2-1-2-3	46	Check ROM copyright notice
2-1-2-4	47	Initialize manager for PCI options ROMs
2-1-3-1	48	Check video configuration against CMOS
2-1-3-2	49	Initialize PCI bus and devices
2-1-3-3	4A	Initialize all video adapters in system
2-1-4-1	4C	Shadow video BIOS ROM
2-1-4-3	4E	Display copyright notice
2-2-1-1	50	Display CPU type and speed
2-2-1-3	52	Test keyboard
2-2-2-1	54	Set key click if enabled
2-2-2-3	56	Enable keyboard
2-2-3-1	58	Test for unexpected interrupts

TABLE 2.6 Beep and POST Codes for the Phoenix 4.0 BIOS (*Continued*)

Beep	POST	Meaning
2-2-3-3	5A	Display prompt "Press F2 to enter Setup"
2-2-4-1	5C	Test RAM between 512 and 640K
2-3-1-1	60	Test expanded memory
2-3-1-3	62	Test extended memory address lines
2-3-2-1	64	Jump to UserPatch1
2-3-2-3	66	Configure advanced cache registers
2-3-3-1	68	Enable external and CPU caches
2-3-3-3	6A	Display external cache size
2-3-4-1	6C	Display shadow message
2-3-4-3	6E	Display nondisposable segments
2-4-1-1	70	Display error messages
2-4-1-3	72	Check for configuration errors
2-4-2-1	74	Test real-time clock
2-4-2-3	76	Check for keyboard errors
2-4-4-1	7C	Set up hardware interrupts vectors
2-4-4-3	7E	Test coprocessor if present
3-1-1-1	80	Disable on-board I/O ports
3-1-1-3	82	Detect and install external RS232 ports
3-1-2-1	84	Detect and install external parallel ports
3-1-2-3	86	Reinitialize onboard I/O ports
3-1-3-1	88	Initialize BIOS data area
3-1-3-3	8A	Initialize extended BIOS data area
3-1-4-1	8C	Initialize floppy controller
3-2-1-1	90	Initialize hard disk controller
3-2-1-2	91	Initialize local-bus hard disk controller
3-2-1-3	92	Jump to UserPatch2
3-2-2-1	94	Disable A20 address line
3-2-2-3	96	Clear huge ES segment register
3-2-3-1	98	Search for option ROMs
3-2-3-3	9A	Shadow option ROMs
3-2-4-1	9C	Set up Power Management
3-2-4-3	9E	Enable hardware interrupts
3-3-1-1	A0	Set time of day
3-3-1-3	A2	Check key lock
3-3-3-1	A8	Erase F2 prompt
3-3-3-3	AA	Scan for F2 key stroke
3-3-4-1	AC	Enter Setup
3-3-4-3	AE	Clear in-POST flag
3-4-1-1	B0	Check for errors
3-4-1-3	B2	POST done—prepare to boot operating system
3-4-2-1	B4	One beep
3-4-2-3	B6	Check password (optional)
3-4-3-1	B8	Clear global descriptor table
3-4-4-1	BC	Clear parity checkers

TABLE 2.6 Beep and POST Codes for the Phoenix 4.0 BIOS
(*Continued*)

Beep	POST	Meaning
3-4-4-3	BE	Clear screen (optional)
3-4-4-4	BF	Check virus and backup reminders
4-1-1-1	C0	Try to boot with INT 19
4-2-1-1	D0	Interrupt handler error
4-2-1-3	D2	Unknown interrupt error
4-2-2-1	D4	Pending interrupt error
4-2-2-3	D6	Initialize option ROM error
4-2-3-1	D8	Shutdown error
4-2-3-3	DA	Extended block move
4-2-4-1	DC	Shutdown 10 error
4-3-1-3	E2	Initialize the motherboard chipset
4-3-1-4	E3	Initialize refresh counter
4-3-2-1	E4	Check for forced Flash
4-3-2-2	E5	Check HW status of ROM
4-3-2-3	E6	BIOS ROM OK
4-3-2-4	E7	Do a complete RAM test
4-3-3-1	E8	Do OEM initialization
4-3-3-2	E9	Initialize interrupt controller
4-3-3-3	EA	Read in bootstrap code
4-3-3-4	EB	Initialize all vectors
4-3-4-1	EC	Boot the Flash program
4-3-4-2	ED	Initialize the boot device
4-3-4-3	EE	Boot code read OK

you insert a POST reader in an open ISA slot and allow the PC to boot, you'll see each POST code flashed to the two 7-segment LED displays on that card. The *last* code to be displayed before the system halts is likely to be the point of failure on your motherboard. Table 2.6 also shows the POST codes for a Phoenix BIOS. Suppose you see a POST code of E2. This means that BIOS was unable to initialize the motherboard's chipset for some reason, and the motherboard is defective.

Motherboard repairs.   Although you can easily replace the add-on items like CPUs, SIMMs, and cache, there is very little that you can do about a defective motherboard—other than to replace the motherboard outright.

Completing the Initial Assembly

Of course, you still cannot boot your new PC yet. You'll need to install the video system, input device(s), and floppy drive before you're able to start the system for the first time.

Step 4: Video system installation

Your next objective should be to prepare the video controller and monitor. This is generally an easy process, but you'll need to pay attention to your options regarding the motherboard and video ports.

Using the motherboard's video port.   If your motherboard already has a video port attached to it, your video system is already installed. All you have to do is attach your monitor to the video port and away you go. Check the motherboard's documentation to be sure that the on-board video controller is enabled. There should also be a disk included with your motherboard that contains the video driver for Windows 95 (put the disk aside for now). Of course, the advantage to using your motherboard's video controller is simplicity—you avoid the cost and installation hassles of a separate video card.

Disabling the motherboard's video port.   You may decide to use another video controller with your PC. This is a common decision that is usually made when the on-board video system does not offer the resolutions, color depths, scanning rates, or 3-D/MPEG performance that you want. Before adding an expansion video board, be sure to *disable* any on-board video controller. This is typically accomplished by setting a single jumper on the motherboard or changing a configuration setting in the CMOS Setup. You should then be able to install the new video controller into an open expansion slot (usually a PCI slot) and install the new drivers. The new video board will come with its own driver disk. You won't need it for DOS, but keep it handy for Windows 95.

> **NOTE:** Some motherboards do not properly disable their on-board video controllers. This allows a hardware conflict between the on-board video controller and the expansion video board. If you have a choice between a motherboard with or without on-board video, choose the one without. Otherwise, you may need a BIOS upgrade to correct the problem.

Installing a video controller.   Insert the video controller board into an available bus slot (usually a PCI slot as in Fig 2.5). In most cases, you should not have to adjust any jumpers on the video board, and hardware conflicts are rare except for BIOS address space (we'll compensate for this when configuring the system later). See that the video board is inserted completely into the slot and then secure the board's metal support bracket with a screw. No additional cabling is required between the video controller and motherboard.

Connecting the monitor.   Once the video controller is installed, attach the video cable from the monitor to the video port. Remember to secure the screws that hold the monitor cable in place. Loose cables can result in intermittent video or other severe image distortion.

Choosing resolutions.   When your system powers up for the first time, it will do so in the DOS mode using

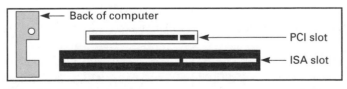

Figure 2.5   PCI versus ISA slots.

a floppy disk (and later with a DOS-formatted hard drive). At this point, you do not need to worry about software driver installation—that will come later with the installation of Windows 95. However, now would be a good time to familiarize yourself with the resolutions and color depths that are available for your particular card so that you can select the optimum resolution. Remember that the resolution must be *within* the range allowed by the monitor. "Overdriving" the monitor by selecting a higher resolution can damage the monitor. Table 2.7 lists the resolutions and color depths for a Matrox Millennium video card.

Video troubleshooting.   Video boards are usually very reliable items, and there are few *hardware* failures. The most frequent problems come during installation. The video board must be seated evenly and completely in its bus slot. Otherwise, the display will remain blank, and you'll probably hear a beep code indicating a video failure. In that case, just turn off your power and reseat the video card.

It is far more common to experience problems with video drivers under Windows 95. Either the wrong driver is being used, or the driver is outdated or buggy. In most cases, updating the video driver will correct those issues. In other cases, the card's video BIOS or the motherboard's BIOS must be updated. If you encounter video problems under Windows or Windows 95, check with the video manufacturer to see if any fixes are available.

Other video problems come from driving the monitor incorrectly. Remember that if you attempt to use a resolution or refresh rate that the monitor is not capable of, you will get severe image distortion and perhaps even damage the monitor itself.

Upgrading a video controller.   Later on, you may choose to replace or upgrade your video card. Video controller upgrades can be accomplished with a simple exchange

TABLE 2.7 Resolutions and Color Depths for a Matrox Millennium Video Card

Resolutions	Maximum 2-D color depths				Resolutions	Maximum 3-D color depths			
	2 Mbyte	4 Mbyte	8 Mbyte			2 Mbyte	4 Mbyte	8 Mbyte
1600 × 1200	256	65K	16.7K		1600 × 1200			256
1280 × 1024	256	16.7M	16.7M		1280 × 1024		256	65K
1152 × 882	65K	16.7M	16.7M		1152 × 882		256	65K
1024 × 768	65K	16.7M	16.7M		1024 × 768		256	16.7M
800 × 600	16.7M	16.7M	16.7M		800 × 600	256	65K	16.7M
640 × 480	16.7M	16.7M	16.7M		640 × 480	65K	16.7M	16.7M

of the controller board. You will then need to identify the new hardware with Windows 95 and install the correct Windows 95 drivers. With PnP video cards, this hardware identification and software installation is initiated automatically. With non-PnP video cards, you can start the new identification process by starting Windows 95 in the Safe Mode and then using the *Add New Hardware* wizard to register the new hardware.

> **NOTE:** If you also upgrade your monitor under Windows 95, you may need to enter the new monitor type within the *Display Properties* dialog.

Windows 3.1x presents an additional wrinkle. You need to switch your current video driver to standard VGA (640×480×16) *before* installing the new video card. Otherwise, Windows 3.1x will try to initialize with the current video driver and probably will not even boot. Once the new video card is installed under Windows 3.1x, you can install the new drivers. It may be necessary to add a memory exclusion to your SYSTEM.INI file, such as

```
EMMEXCLUDE = A000-C7FF
```

Under DOS, you may also need to add a corresponding memory exclusion to your EMM386 command line under CONFIG.SYS in order to prevent other devices from competing with the new video board's memory space requirements, such as:

```
DEVICE = C:\WINDOWS\EMM386.EXE RAM I = A000-C7FF
```

Step 5: Keyboard installation

By now, your system is starting to take shape. Go ahead and attach the keyboard to the keyboard connector at the case. If the keyboard connector is actually fixed to the motherboard, you should be all set. If not, take another look and make sure that the keyboard connector cable is attached properly to the motherboard. For cases with a keyboard lock feature, insert the key and select the unlocked position.

AT versus PS/2 connections.   There are two different styles of keyboard connector: Baby AT (a five-pin connector) and PS/2 (a six-pin connector). Both connectors carry exactly the same signals and can be matched easily through the use of a keyboard adapter. Ideally, the keyboard connector should match the keyboard connector on the case—a mechanical adapter can wear out and can cause keyboard problems. If it does not, you'll need to exchange your keyboard for the correct connector type or buy a keyboard adapter from your local computer store.

Keyboard troubleshooting.   Keyboards are essentially mechanical devices, and they can and do wear out. Keep the keyboard clean by periodically dusting with a can of compressed air (this is more important in dusty environments such as homes). If a key sticks or fails to make contact reliably, you can gently remove the key cap with a key removal tool, or use a straightened paper clip bent like a U with the tips bent inward to face each other. Insert both tips under the key cap and ease the cap straight up. You can then clean the key contacts with good-quality electrical contact cleaner. If problems continue (or other keyboard errors are generated), replace the keyboard outright.

Upgrading the keyboard.   Keyboards can be replaced or upgraded simply by disconnecting the old unit and attaching the new one. No further action is required from a hardware standpoint. However, many new keyboards are being equipped with special features like Windows 95 keys, page scanners, or integrated pointing devices. These may demand some additional installation steps and will *certainly* need software drivers under DOS and Windows 95.

Step 6: Floppy drive system installation

Next, you must establish the floppy drive controller system in your PC. If the motherboard already provides floppy drive support (as most do now), you are all set to go. Otherwise, you'll need to install a drive controller board into an available expansion slot (usually PCI). Once the drive controller is established, you can install the floppy drive and boot the system for the first time.

Using the motherboard's floppy controller. If your motherboard already provides a 34-pin floppy disk controller (usually marked FDD for Floppy Disk Drive), you can simply connect your floppy drive(s) to the motherboard. Check your motherboard's documentation and see that the floppy drive controller is enabled. Take your floppy drive cable and attach the controller end to the 34-pin FDD header on the motherboard. The little red or blue stripe down one side of the cable is always regarded as pin 1. Make sure the pin 1 side of the cable is pointed to the side of the 34-pin header marked 1/2.

Disabling the motherboard's floppy controller. If you choose to use an expansion drive controller board (often chosen to provide EIDE support for older motherboards), the controller will often provide *both* floppy drive and hard drive controller ports. If you plan to use an expansion drive controller, you must refer to the motherboard's documentation and *disable* the onboard floppy drive (and hard drive) controller ports.

> **NOTE:** Because virtually all new motherboards support good-quality floppy drive interfaces, use the motherboard's drive controller ports if possible.

Installing a drive controller. Floppy and hard drive resources are very standardized, so you should rarely need to move any jumpers on the drive controller board. If the motherboard BIOS already provides EIDE support, you may simply need to disable the EIDE drive controller's local BIOS (usually accomplished through a single jumper on the controller itself). If you're installing a controller specifically to provide EIDE support, leave the controller's on-board BIOS enabled.

Next, simply insert the drive controller into an available expansion slot. See that the drive controller is inserted completely into the slot and then secure the board's metal support bracket with a screw. No additional cabling is required between the drive controller and motherboard.

Take your floppy drive cable and attach the controller end to the 34-pin FDD header on the drive controller board. The little red or blue stripe down one side of the cable is always regarded as pin 1. Make sure the pin 1 side of the cable is pointed to the side of the 34-pin header marked 1/2.

Installing the floppy drive. Mount the floppy drive into an external drive bay and then secure the drive into place with four screws. Be sure not to strip or overtighten the screws, or you can warp the drive frame and cause drive problems. Take the floppy drive cable and connect the *end-most* connector (the end *after* the cable flip) to the 34-pin header on the floppy drive. Again, be sure that pin 1 on the cable is aligned with the side of the signal connector on the floppy drive marked 1/2. This drive will become drive A: on your system. Finally, take one 4-pin power connector from the power supply and connect it to your floppy drive.

> **NOTE:** Insert your bootable floppy disk into the floppy drive *now*.

Troubleshooting a floppy system. Drive controllers are remarkably robust items (so long as the motherboard is running properly). However, they can and do fail. If you encounter a sudden failure of *all* your floppy and hard drives and the drives check out on other systems (or new drives don't fix the problem), chances are that the controller has failed. Your only course then is to replace the controller outright. If you had been using the motherboard's drive controller, you'll need to disable the on-board drive controller and install a stand-alone controller to take its place.

Typical floppy drive problems come from a lack of maintenance (dirty Read/Write, or R/W heads), a damaged signal cable, poor-quality media, or power problems. The drive itself can fail due to wear and tear, and it is always more economical to replace a floppy drive outright than to repair it. The general order in floppy troubleshooting is this:

- Check the media (try a different disk)
- Clean the drive
- Check the power
- Check the signal cable
- Replace the drive
- Replace the drive controller

Upgrading a drive controller. In most cases, replacing one drive controller with another is a relatively straightforward operation. You must disconnect the drive cables (floppy and hard drive) from the controller and remove the old controller. Check the jumpers on the new controller to see that the board is properly configured and then install the new controller in an available bus slot. You can then reattach the drive cables (watch out for the orientations of pin 1).

Upgrading a floppy drive. Few people bother to upgrade a floppy drive unless they are working with an older 5.25- or 3.5-in double-density (720-kbyte) drive. The standard floppy drive today is 3.5-in high-density (1.44 Mbyte). Generally, you simply must replace a defective floppy drive. Disconnect the power and signal cables, unbolt the floppy drive, and then slide the old drive out of its drive bay. Insert the new floppy drive and bolt it into place—remember not to overtighten the screws—and then attach the power and signal cable (be careful to check the orientation of pin 1).

If you install a different floppy drive, you'll need to update the floppy drive designation in CMOS Setup before the system will boot properly. Of course, if your boot order in CMOS Setup is set as C:/A:, the system may ignore the floppy and just boot directly from the hard drive, and you will not see a floppy error until you try to actually use it.

Step 7: Initial testing

That's it for this part of the assembly. Now, we're going to fire up the new system and test its operation. Don't get nervous—you've been doing well. The steps below will take you through the essential testing protocol. You might wonder why we're testing so early in the assembly process. There's one reason—simplicity. The less there is in your system, the easier it will be to isolate problems. As you become more proficient at assembling a PC, you might choose to skip this interim step, but for now, let's prove out the motherboard, video system, and floppy drive system and pay a visit to our friendly neighborhood DOS prompt:

- Remove any tools, screws, clips, or other stuff from the case area. Make sure that children and household pets are clear.

- Attach the AC line cord to the AC outlet.

- Also turn the monitor on (turn the brightness up to maximum).

Power up.   No excuses—flip the switch. You should expect several things to happen:

- The power supply fan, case fan(s), and CPU fan should start spinning.

- The monitor should flicker a bit, but you should see "raster" (that faint, dark gray background haze on the CRT). This usually indicates that the video system is working.

- After a moment, you will probably see a BIOS banner on screen, and the memory test will probably count up.

> **NOTE:** If any of these events do not occur, turn your power off, unplug the AC line cord, and refer to the troubleshooting steps below.

Configure the CMOS Setup. On your first power-up, you should *expect* to see an error message indicating that the system's CMOS Setup does not match the equipment found (or some other Setup-related error). Press the appropriate key combination to start your Setup routine and then enter the correct parameters for your system. You should expect to enter your floppy drive as the *only* drive present—other drives should be marked "None" or "Not Installed." Also make sure that the correct amount of RAM and cache are listed. Set the date and time. You may want to refer to the motherboard manual to set the other CMOS optimizations. If you're not sure what they mean, refer to the CMOS Setup reference in App. A.

> **NOTE:** If you encounter any problems with your video, try disabling the advanced video features such as Video Shadow, Video Cache, Pallet Snoop, Decouple Refresh, or Hidden Refresh. Disable one feature at a time and see if it helps stabilize your system.

Set the boot order in CMOS. Another thing to check in CMOS Setup is the drive boot order. By default, the order is C:/A:, which will generate an error if the C:

drive is not present. Change the boot order to A:/C: so that the system will boot from the floppy drive if possible.

> **NOTE:** Save your changes to the CMOS Setup and reboot the system.

Boot from the floppy drive. At this point, you should be able to boot the system completely from your floppy drive and boot disk. After the BIOS POST, you will see a message such as "Starting MS-DOS" (or "Starting Windows 95" if you're using a Windows 95 start-up disk) and then the floppy drive light should come on. A minute later, you should see the A:\>prompt.

Congratulations! The first part of your construction is essentially complete.

Test the CMOS Setup. One final test before you revel in your achievement. Turn off the system, go make yourself some coffee, and then come back and turn the system on again. You need to see if your CMOS settings will hold after power is turned off. If the system boots again as expected, you're done with this section. If you see the same CMOS error message you noticed when you first turned the system on, your CMOS settings have been lost. You may have inserted the battery backward or mis-set the jumper that switches between the on-board battery and external battery pack. Check them—check them now and then reenter your CMOS settings and repeat this step. Do not proceed until the system will *hold* your CMOS Setup values.

Initial troubleshooting. No matter how much care you take, there are times when things simply do not work properly. In most cases, you'll find that the problem is something simple—you put a cable on backward, forgot a cable connection, or neglected to install something important. Don't worry—it happens to us all. Start by checking some of the basics:

- Make sure that the AC line cord is plugged in properly.

- Make sure the power switch is *on* (and that the voltage selector switch is set properly).

- Make sure the two motherboard power connectors are attached to their proper points on the motherboard (turn the power *off* first before fiddling with these).

- Make sure that there are no screws or metal parts on the motherboard that may be shorting things out.

- Make sure that the monitor is plugged in, turned on, and securely attached to the video port.

Some of the more common troubleshooting issues are outlined below:

Symptom 1: System is dead.   This is a common problem with new system builds and is almost always the result of a connection problem. The power supply cooling fan probably comes on, but there is no activity in the system.

- Check the motherboard power connectors (be sure to turn the power *off* before fiddling with these).

- Make sure that none of the metal standoffs mounting the motherboard are shorting out any circuit traces (this should not happen if you used nonconductive plastic washers during your construction).

- Make sure that your video controller is enabled and installed properly.

- Check the power supply—measure each of the voltage levels powering the motherboard. If any voltages appear low or absent, the power supply may be defective and should be exchanged.

- Replace the motherboard. At this point, that's all you really have left.

Symptom 2: You hear beeps. This is another common problem with new system builds. When the PC starts, the BIOS runs a self-diagnostic test to see that all of the expected equipment is available and responding. If a major error is detected on the motherboard, the BIOS will generate a series of beeps (a beep code) that indicates the error. Every BIOS uses its own set of beep codes, so you will need to refer to the motherboard documentation to determine the precise failure.

Before proceeding any further, check to be sure that your video controller board and all SIMMs are seated properly in their slots. If not, power down the system and reseat the video controller. If there is also a video controller on the motherboard, see that it has been disabled properly. Also try reseating the SIMMs. If beeps continue, you will almost certainly have to replace the motherboard.

Symptom 3: Initialization hang-ups. It is also common for the system to accomplish its self-testing properly but stall or hang up when attempting to actually boot the operating system (from the floppy drive in this case). If you're using a stand-alone drive controller, check to be sure that your drive controller board is seated properly in its bus slot before proceeding any further. If it is not, power down the system and reseat the drive controller. If there is also a drive controller on the motherboard, see that it has been disabled properly. Also check that your floppy drive has been cabled and powered correctly. Finally, check the system CMOS Setup to see that your floppy drive is configured correctly.

Symptom 4: Intermittent stalls or reboots. If the system appears to reboot spontaneously, you have a short circuit—probably between the motherboard wire traces and one or more metal standoffs or screws (bet you wish you'd used those plastic washers now, hummmmm?). If the system stalls after some period of time (and needs to be turned off for a while before it will run again), your

CPU is probably overheating. Check that the CPU heat sink/fan is attached securely and has a thin layer of thermal grease to aid heat transfer. Also see that the CPU fan is running correctly (some budget heat sink/fans are unreliable). You may replace troublesome heat sink/fans outright.

Symptom 5: The floppy drive *cannot* be located. The drive light remains on continuously. The floppy drive just spins and spins but doesn't read the disk. In every case that I have ever heard of, one end of the floppy drive's signal cable has been inserted backward. Take a moment and double-check the alignment of pin 1 at both ends of the signal cable.

Symptom 6: You see *normal* system activity but there is no video. Chances are that the monitor is not on or is not connected properly to the video board. Make sure that the monitor is plugged in and turned on. This type of oversight is really more common than you might think. Check to make sure that the monitor works (you may want to try the monitor on a known-good system). If the monitor fails on a known-good system, replace the monitor. Trace the monitor cable to its connection at the video board and verify that the connector is inserted securely. It is possible that the video board has failed. Try a known good monitor. If the problem persists, replace the video board.

Finishing the Assembly

Even though your system is now bootable, you can understand why it would be terribly limited with just a single floppy drive installed. Modern PCs use hard drives and a selection of multimedia hardware to round out the system's capabilities. In this chapter, we'll finish up the physical construction of your new PC with the installation and preparation of a hard drive, sound board, CD-ROM drive, and a few other peripherals. Let's jump right into hard drive installation.

> **NOTE:** Before you proceed with any of the steps in this chapter, make sure that all of the hardware installed in Sec. 2 is secure and operating correctly.

Setting Up the Hard Drive

Once your system is booting from the floppy drive, the next step is to get your hard drive up and running. You'll need the hard drive in order to hold the real-mode drivers and start-up files needed to run your other drives and devices that must be installed before Windows 95.

Step 8: Hard drive system installation

You must establish the hard drive controller system in your PC. If the motherboard already provides hard drive support (as most do now), you are all set to go. Otherwise, you'll need to install a drive controller board into an available expansion slot (usually PCI). Once the drive controller is established, we can install the hard drive and prepare it for use. For the purposes of this book, we'll assume that you're using EIDE devices unless SCSI devices are mentioned specifically.

Using the motherboard's hard drive controller. If your motherboard already provides an EIDE 40-pin hard disk controller (usually marked HDD), you can simply connect your hard drive to the motherboard. Check your motherboard's documentation and see that the hard drive controller is *enabled.* Take your hard drive cable (careful, it looks like the floppy cable, but there are 40 pins instead of 34, and there's no flip in the cable) and attach the controller end to the 40-pin HDD header on the motherboard. The little red or blue stripe down one side of the cable is always regarded as pin 1. Make sure the pin 1 side of the cable is pointed to the side of the 40-pin header marked 1/2.

Chances are that your drive controller (motherboard *or* expansion board) provides *two* channels: a primary EIDE channel, which supports two EIDE devices (typically large hard drives), and a secondary IDE channel designed to support slower IDE devices (such as older hard drives or ATAPI devices such as CD-ROM drives). When installing the hard drive, make sure to start with the *primary* 40-pin channel—our first hard drive is going to be bootable.

Disabling the motherboard's hard drive controller. If you choose to use an expansion drive controller board (often chosen if the motherboard does not support EIDE), the controller will often provide both floppy drive and hard drive controller ports. If you plan to use an expansion drive controller, you must refer to the motherboard's documentation and *disable* the on-board hard drive controller ports. If you're already using a floppy controller on the motherboard, you must *disable* the floppy port on the controller card; otherwise, you'll have a hardware conflict. As an alternative, you can disable the motherboard's floppy controller and move the floppy cable to the controller card's floppy port.

> **NOTE:** With virtually all new motherboards supporting high-performance EIDE interfaces, use the motherboard's drive controller ports if possible.

Installing a drive controller. Hard drive resources are *very* standardized, so you should rarely need to move any jumpers on the drive controller board unless you need to disable unused ports. If the motherboard BIOS already provides EIDE support, you may simply need to disable the EIDE drive controller's local BIOS (usually accomplished through a single jumper on the controller itself).

Next, simply insert the drive controller into an available expansion slot (usually a PCI card slot). See that the drive controller is inserted evenly and completely into the slot and then secure the board's metal support bracket with a screw. No additional cabling is required between the drive controller and motherboard.

> **NOTE:** If you decide to use the motherboard's floppy drive port but use an expansion drive controller for your hard drive, be sure to *disable* the floppy drive port on the drive controller board.

Take your hard drive cable and attach the controller end to the primary 40-pin HDD header on the drive controller board (we'll leave the secondary channel open for now). The little red or blue stripe down one side of the cable is always regarded as pin 1. Make sure the pin 1 side of the cable is pointed to the side of the 34-pin header marked 1/2.

Installing a SCSI controller.   Motherboards and BIOS support floppy drives and EIDE devices. If you plan to use SCSI drives (either instead of or in addition to EIDE drives), you'll need to install an SCSI controller board. A few motherboards support a native SCSI interface, but these are rare—and often are supplanted by a high-performance SCSI controller card anyway.

SCSI controller installation requires you to configure the controller's IRQ, I/O address range, and SCSI BIOS address range before installing the card. The SCSI BIOS is used only to support SCSI hard drives. If you will *not* be adding SCSI hard drives, you can *disable* the SCSI BIOS. Be very careful when configuring the card to avoid using resources used by other devices (such as the floppy controller). This can easily result in hardware conflicts that will disrupt SCSI operation. Once the card is configured, simply insert the SCSI controller into an available expansion slot (usually a PCI card slot). See that the SCSI controller is inserted evenly and completely into the slot and then secure the board's metal support bracket with a screw. No additional cabling is required between the SCSI controller and motherboard.

Take your SCSI signal cable and attach one end to the 50- or 68-pin header on the SCSI controller board—all SCSI devices in your system will be daisy chained to this SCSI cable. The little red or blue stripe down one side of the cable is always regarded as pin 1. Make sure the pin 1 side of the cable is pointed to the side of the 50- or 68-pin header marked 1/2.

SCSI versus EIDE performance.   As discussed in Sec. 1, both SCSI and EIDE interfaces are quite good, and

either will be an excellent addition to your PC platform. EIDE performance is not as good as SCSI, but it
is very convenient and inexpensive. SCSI is more
expensive and is very controller dependent, but it is
most effective for top performance (especially in true
multitasking systems). Table 3.1 lists the data transfer rates for SCSI bus architectures, and Table 3.2
outlines the data transfer rates for IDE/EIDE interfaces. Although high-end SCSI interfaces can easily
exceed 20 Mbytes/s, the average general-purpose 16-bit
SCSI-2 interface is about equivalent to a PIO Mode 4
EIDE interface.

TABLE 3.1 SCSI Data Transfer Rates

SCSI bus clock (MHz)	8 bit (50-wire data cable) (Mbytes/s)	16 bit (68-wire data cable, wide SCSI) (Mbytes/s)
5 (SCSI 1)	5	N/A
10 (Fast SCSI, SCSI-2)	10	20
20 (Fast-20, Ultra SCSI)	20	40
40 (Fast-40, Ultra-2 SCSI)	40	80

TABLE 3.2 IDE/EIDE Data Transfer Rates

Mode	Transfer rate (Mbytes/s)
Possible transfer rates of an IDE bus (ATA)	
Single-word DMA 0	2.1
PIO Mode 0	3.3
Single-word DMA 1, multiword DMA 0	4.2
PIO Mode 1	5.2
PIO Mode 2, single-word DMA 2	8.3
Possible transfer rates of an EIDE bus (ATA-2)	
PIO Mode 3	11.1
Multiword DMA 1	13.3
PIO Mode 4, multiword DMA 2	16.6
Possible transfer rates of Ultra-ATA (Ultra DMA/33)	
Multiword DMA 3	33.3

Hard drive geometry.   Before doing anything else, locate the documentation for your drive that lists the drive's geometry figures. BIOS requires this data in order to know just how big the drive is and how to access it correctly. These figures may also be listed on the drive itself (manufacturers are getting a lot better at this). No matter *where* these numbers are located, write them on a piece of paper and tape that paper to your case or user manual—do it *now*. There are usually five key parameters (take a glance back at Table 1.4 to compare some current drive parameters):

- Heads
- Cylinders (or tracks)
- Sectors (per track)
- Write precompensation (or WPre)
- Landing zone (or LZ)

> **NOTE:** Virtually all current hard drives and BIOS support the autodetection of EIDE hard drives. During start-up, BIOS will query the hard drive, which will return the drive geometry figures automatically. This simplifies drive installation a bit but is not always perfect. Older hard drives or older BIOS may not support autodetection properly. You should still locate and highlight the drive geometry to have it on hand in the event that autodetection fails (see "Dealing with huge EIDE hard drive problems," below).

Configuring the hard drive.   An IDE/EIDE controller port will support up to two drives—a *primary* drive (traditionally called the master) and a *secondary* drive (called the slave). Every hard drive has several jumpers to define its role in this drive order (Fig. 3.1). The primary drive will usually be C:, and the secondary drive will be D:. You can set the drive in one of three ways:

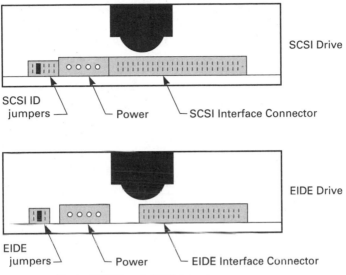

SCSI Drive

SCSI ID
jumpers ⎦ ⎣ Power ⎦ ⎣ SCSI Interface Connector

EIDE Drive

EIDE
jumpers ⎦ ⎣ Power ⎦ ⎣ EIDE Interface Connector

Figure 3.1 Typical EIDE and SCSI drive jumpers.

- The primary (or master) drive in a single drive system.

- The primary (or master) drive in a dual drive system.

- The secondary (or slave) drive.

  NOTE: Some of the newer drives also provide a setting called CSEL, CS, or Cable Select. As a rule, you should avoid using this setting and configure the drive specifically as a primary or secondary device.

SCSI hard drives are identified a bit differently. Rather than a master/slave relationship, each device on the SCSI chain is assigned an SCSI ID number between 0 and 7. The SCSI controller is typically assigned to ID7 by default. Your first (bootable) SCSI hard drive is jumpered as ID0, and a second SCSI hard drive is jumpered as ID1.

Mounting the hard drive. Mount the hard drive into an available drive bay (it can be an internal or external bay) and then secure the drive into place with *four* screws. Do not use less than four screws because the drive may be subject to excessive vibrations that might shorten its working life. Be sure not to strip or overtighten the screws—this can warp the drive frame just slightly and result in drive failures.

Take the hard drive cable attached to the EIDE controller port and connect the end-most connector to the 40-pin header on the hard drive. For SCSI drives, take the 50- or 68-pin cable attached to the SCSI controller and connect the end-most connector in the cable to the first SCSI hard drive. Again, be sure that pin 1 on the cable is aligned with the side of the signal connector on the hard drive marked 1/2. Finally, take one 4-pin power connector from the power supply and connect it to your hard drive.

> **NOTE:** The SCSI chain must also be *terminated* with resistors. By default, the SCSI controller is usually terminated. If your SCSI hard drive is the last device on the SCSI chain, make sure to terminate the drive properly. Improper SCSI termination can result in poor drive performance, data corruption, and drive errors.

Configuring the hard drive in CMOS. The hard drive will *not* work the very first time you fire up the PC. You will have to identify the drive to the system and prepare the drive with an operating system like DOS. Start by identifying the drive to your system through CMOS. Power up the system with the boot disk (you'll probably see an error message because of the new hard drive) and enter your CMOS Setup routine the way you did when setting up the floppy drive (usually by using <F1> or some other keys).

Once the CMOS Setup starts, find the entries for your hard drive and enter the drive geometry that you recorded a few paragraphs ago (Fig. 3.2). Even though your drive and BIOS probably support autodetection,

Primary IDE Master ST32140A

IDE Device Configuration	Auto Configured	**F1**	Help
		ESC	Back
Number of Cylinders	4095	**Enter**	Select
Number of Heads	16		
Number of Sectors	63	**>**	Previous Item
Maximum Capacity	2016 MB	**>**	Next Item
		>	Select Menu
IDE Translation Mode	Auto Detected		
Multiple Sector Setting	Auto Detected	**F5**	Setup Defaults
Fast Programmed I/O Modes	Auto Detected	**F6**	Previous Values
		F10	Save & Exit

Figure 3.2 Entering hard drive geometry figures.

you should enter the geometry values manually. If you cannot enter the values manually, go ahead and use the autodetect feature. Be sure to save your changes and then reboot the system with your bootable disk.

SCSI hard drives cause a bit of a wrinkle. You should *not* enter SCSI geometry values in the CMOS Setup routine (this assumes that IDE/EIDE drives are being used). The SCSI BIOS will autoidentify the SCSI drive(s). If you're using SCSI hard drives instead of IDE/EIDE hard drives, be sure that the drive entries in your CMOS Setup are marked "none" or "not installed."

Preparing the hard drive. At this point, the system boots to the A:> prompt, but the hard drive is still not recognized. Go ahead, try it—type C: and press <Enter>. You'll see an error message like "Invalid drive letter." Although the PC *hardware* sees the drive, DOS does not. Now let's prepare that drive for service. There are three steps: partitioning, formatting, and "SYSing."

Partition the drive. Remember that FDISK utility you copied to that boot disk? Run that utility and create at least one logical DOS partition. Remember to make this primary partition *active* and *bootable*. Partitioning creates a logical volume that DOS can recognize. If your hard drive is larger than 2.1 Gbytes, create one partition *up to* 2.1 Gbytes and then make a *second* partition with the remaining space. FDISK will support up to four partitions on a single physical hard drive. I won't describe FDISK too much here because there are entire books written on DOS. It actually should take no more than a moment to create each partition. Keep in mind that you only need one primary DOS partition to be active in order to get the drive running. You could create additional partitions later with any remaining space, but it is usually easier to fully partition the drive from the beginning. If you find yourself repartitioning a lot, take a look at the Partition Magic utility from PowerQuest (*www.powerquest.com*).

One of the most frequent questions I come across has to do with partition size and wasted space. DOS, Windows, and Windows 95 use a File Allocation Table (FAT) type of file system, where sectors on the drive are grouped into clusters. There is a fixed number of bits available to specify each cluster—for the FAT 16 file system, there can be 2^{16} (two to the sixteenth power), or 65,536 clusters. Because the number of clusters is fixed, larger drives *must* use larger clusters. The problem is that files cannot share a cluster, so small files (or portions of files) take up entire clusters. This results in wasted space (called *slack space*). In actual practice, the amount of space wasted by today's files is rather small (unless you work with a large number of *very* small files), but some PC users choose to reduce slack space by creating smaller partitions. Table 3.3 compares partition and cluster sizes. With the introduction of the Windows 95 Original Equipment Manufacture (OEM) Service Release 2 (OSR 2), a FAT 32 architecture is available that allows 2^{28} clusters—this supports an 8-Gbyte partition with clusters of only 4 kbytes. Once FAT 32

TABLE 3.3 Partition Sizes versus Cluster Sizes

Partition size	Cluster size (kbytes)
1 to 2 Gbytes	32
<1 Gbyte	16
<512 Mbytes	8
<256 Mbytes	4
<128 Mbytes	2

enters common use, slack space worries should ease considerably.

Multiple drives and the drive letter order.   A funny thing often happens when two physical hard drives are installed in the same system and each drive uses two or more partitions. The first partition of the primary drive is C:, the first partition of the secondary drive is D:, and the remaining partitions of the primary drive are assigned letters (i.e., E:, F:, G:, and so on). The remaining partitions of the secondary drive are assigned letters (i.e., H:, I:, J:, and such). This happens because DOS assigns drive letters to primary DOS partitions first and *then* to extended DOS partitions. If you create a primary DOS partition on more then one hard drive, DOS will assign letters to them first *before* assigning letters to the remaining partitions. This certainly doesn't harm the drives, but it can cause a bit of confusion unless you know what's going on. If you want to keep your drive letters in order from drive to drive, create a primary DOS partition on the first drive *only* and use extended DOS partitions for the rest.

> **NOTE:** There's only one disadvantage to using *only* extended DOS partitions on your secondary drive—you can't make that drive bootable if you need to (you'd need to repartition the drive with a primary DOS partition).

Format the drive.   Now use the FORMAT utility you copied to that bootable disk. Run FORMAT:

```
A:\> FORMAT C:  <Enter>
```

This will format the C: partition on your hard drive for DOS. Remember, if you have several partitions on the drive, you will have to format each partition individually. Formatting organizes all the sectors and tracks on the drive to hold DOS information. Formatting may take several minutes depending on the size of your drive. If you want to format the drive and make it bootable at the same time, use the /S switch:

```
A:\> FORMAT C: /S  <Enter>
```

Make the drive bootable.   If you did not use the /S switch with your FORMAT utility, the last step is to make the drive bootable. The SYS utility (which I hope you copied to your bootable floppy disk) will transfer the system files to your primary DOS partition (the C: drive). Use the SYS command:

```
A:> SYS C:  <Enter>
```

Dealing with huge EIDE hard drive problems.   There are known problems autodetecting EIDE drives larger than 4 Gbytes. This is typically because the BIOS doesn't truly support the large number of cylinders that are involved. The drive usually autodetects correctly, but this type of problem typically manifests itself when the system reboots. There are two solutions to this problem. First, you should update your BIOS with a version that will better support huge hard drives. The temporary work-around is to use a translation scheme in the CMOS Setup.

   The first EIDE drives larger than 4 Gbytes appeared on the market in early 1997. These drives seem to work in some systems and not in others. This problem is not due to a bug in the BIOS but is actually an operating system issue—pertaining to all versions of MS-DOS through 6.22. Windows 95 seems to have the same problem. The problem is that DOS cannot handle a translated drive geometry with 256 heads. You may find that these huge hard drives seem to autotype correctly in BIOS, and the problem crops up when trying to partition the drive. The partition may seem to be created properly through FDISK, but the system hangs up when rebooting. Although this is an operating system limitation, it appears that the appropriate way to deal with this problem is to account for it in the system BIOS. Fortunately, there is a temporary work-around to the problem (until you get the BIOS upgraded).

> **NOTE:** You should first verify that you have a new enough version to handle drives *over* 2 Gbytes correctly.

To set up a drive over 4 Gbytes (Table 3.4 lists some sample work-around parameters):

1. Autodetect the drive in CMOS Setup.

2. Manually adjust the number of heads from 16 to 15.

3. Multiply the number of cylinders by 16/15 (rounded down to whole number). Because 16/15 is 1.06667, the simplest way to multiply by 16/15 would be to multiply by 1.06667 (and then round down to a whole number).

TABLE 3.4 Typical Work-around Parameters for Huge Hard Drives

Model	Factory CHS values	Work-around CHS values
Maxtor 85120A	$9924 \times 16 \times 63$	$10585 \times 15 \times 63$
Micropolis 4550A	$9692 \times 16 \times 63$	$10338 \times 15 \times 63$

4. Adjust the number of cylinders to this larger amount.

5. Write down these adjusted values for cylinders, heads, and sectors.

6. Save changes to CMOS and partition and format the drive.

Although this can be considered a *temporary* workaround, there should be no problem with continuing to use a hard drive set up this way. If an updated BIOS version is used at a later date, it should not be necessary to repartition and reformat the drive.

> **NOTE:** The important thing to keep in mind in using the above work-around is that you must keep a record of the translation values used so that they can be reentered if the contents of CMOS RAM are lost or if the drive is moved to another system. Write the values on masking tape, and stick the tape on the drive itself.

Drive translation software. Today's huge hard drives are fully supported by the motherboard BIOS or EIDE controller board BIOS. But you may encounter older hardware that does not provide hardware support for EIDE, and it may not be practical or cost-effective to update the drive controller. In that case, you can use drive translation software (also called overlay software) such as Ontrack's Disk Manager or EZ-Drive. Both of these software solutions install to the drive's master boot record and allow the full capacity of the drive to be utilized even though the hardware may only handle up to 528 Mbytes (a traditional IDE limit).

The advantage of overlay software is convenience— a copy of Disk Manager or EZ-Drive is included on a floppy disk shipped with most new hard drives, and it's free. You could download a copy of EZ-Drive from the Western Digital technical support site (www.wdc.com). Current versions of drive overlay software are also fully compatible with Windows 95, Windows NT, and OS/2. There are very few system penalties with overlay software, although performance is diminished just slightly, and any damage to the overlay file on a hard drive can render the drive's contents inaccessible.

> **NOTE:** Although products like Disk Manager and EZ-Drive are good and reliable pieces of software, do not use overlay software unless it is absolutely necessary.

SCSI drivers. If you choose to work with SCSI systems at all, you're going to need SCSI drivers. You won't need drivers to handle SCSI hard drives because the SCSI BIOS already provides the firmware for that. However, other devices (such as SCSI CD-ROM drives) will need SCSI drivers—a real-mode driver for CONFIG.SYS to support operation under DOS and a protected-mode driver to support operation under Windows 95. For now, you should not have to install any DOS drivers to handle the SCSI hard drive(s).

> **NOTE:** If you forgo the use of real-mode drivers, you will not be able to access the corresponding device while in the DOS mode. This can result in odd drive letter assignments or cause some programs not to work.

Test the hard drive. Now for another moment of truth. After the drive has been prepared for service, remove the floppy disk and reboot the system. If all goes well, you should see a message like "Starting MS-DOS" (or "Starting Windows 95" if you're using a Windows 95 start-up disk); then you will be asked for the date and time—just hit <Enter> both times, and you should see the C:> prompt. Congratulations, the hard drive is running. If you have more than one partition on the drive, try switching to the other logical drives to see that you get the correct prompt.

Dealing with a troublesome hard drive. Hard drive installations are some of the most common and frequent upgrade processes, so you should make it a point to understand the steps involved as clearly as possible. In most cases, the drive should install, partition, and format without a hitch. If things do not go quite so smoothly, there are some checkpoints problems to consider:

- Check the drive power and signal cables.
- Check that the hard drive controller is enabled or installed correctly.
- Check that the drive jumper is set properly.
- Check the CMOS Setup and verify that the correct drive geometry has been entered.
- Change the hard drive.
- Change the drive controller.

Symptom 1: The drive does not spin up. You should hear the drive's spindle motor the moment you turn the PC on (that high "whirring" sound). If you don't, chances are that you just forgot to plug in the power connector (or the connector is not plugged in properly). Turn the PC *off* before plugging in the power connector. If the drive still refuses to spin up, the drive itself may be defective. Try another drive.

Symptom 2: The drive light stays on. If you receive an error from the system indicating something like a Drive Failure or Drive Controller Error and the drive light remains on, chances are that one end of your drive signal cable is installed backward. Check the alignment of pin 1 on each end of the drive cable.

Symptom 3: The hard drive is not recognized. This happens a great deal with new installations. In almost all cases, you've entered the incorrect drive geometry in the CMOS Setup (or forgot to "Save changes and exit"). Check the CMOS Setup again. If problems persist, try another hard drive.

Upgrading a drive controller.   At some point in the future, you may choose to upgrade your existing drive controller. Upgrading a drive controller is not terribly difficult, but there are some important points to remember. First, you're going to remove at least one hard drive cable—and probably one floppy drive cable—from the controller. You can then unbolt the controller board and remove it from the system (if you're upgrading from a motherboard-based controller, remember to *disable* the motherboard's drive controllers). When you have the new controller board ready, plug the hard drive cables into place (remember to check the alignment of pin 1). If you're running the floppy drive(s) from the drive controller, you'll also need to plug the floppy cable into the controller (again, be careful of pin 1). Carefully insert the controller into its card slot, and bolt the board into place. Windows 95 should not need to report the new hardware because IDE/EIDE and floppy controllers are BIOS-supported.

However, SCSI controllers represent a very different set of challenges during an upgrade procedure. Aside from exchanging an SCSI cable and checking for proper termination, the actual physical replacement of the SCSI controller is very straightforward. However, new SCSI controllers will demand a new set of SCSI drivers. This is not such a problem for hard drive setups, but other SCSI devices like CD-ROM drives, scanners, tape drives, and so on, will all require driver updates to accommodate the new controller. Further, SCSI controllers each handle hard drives a bit differently, so updating an SCSI controller may *require* you to reformat your SCSI hard drive(s).

Step 9: Copy the DOS files

Now that your hard drive is working, create a DOS subdirectory, and copy all of the utilities from your bootable floppy disk. This is a temporary measure, and you can delete these files from the hard drive once your final operating system is installed. Once you copy the start-up files, you can put the bootable disk aside. Start by creating the DOS directory:

```
C:\> md dos  <Enter>
```

Then switch to the DOS directory:

```
C:\> cd dos  <Enter>
```

Now copy all the files from your bootable disk to the DOS directory:

```
C:\> copy a:*.* c:  <Enter>
```

Make sure that you have copies of HIMEM.SYS and EMM386.EXE included in the DOS directory (you'll need these when setting up your start-up files). Finally, erase the COMMAND.COM file from your DOS directory. COMMAND.COM was placed in the root directory when you formatted or SYSed the hard drive, and you shouldn't have more than one copy of COMMAND.COM on the drive:

```
C:\> erase command.com  <Enter>
```

Step 10: Create your start-up files

Next, you should create a basic DOS environment to get started with. To do that, let's create a basic CONFIG.SYS and AUTOEXEC.BAT file.

CONFIG.SYS. The CONFIG.SYS file is the perfect vehicle for launching DOS device drivers and assigning other low-level system variables. Make sure you're in the C: drive root directory and then type

```
COPY CON CONFIG.SYS  <Enter>
```

This opens a new file called "CONFIG.SYS." Now type the following:

```
device = c:\dos\himem.sys
device = C:\dos\emm386.exe ram
dos = umb,high
FILES = 50
BUFFERS = 20
^Z
```

If you copied files from a DOS 6.22 system, HIMEM.SYS and EMM386 should have been included, as you saw at the beginning of Sec. 2. If you copied files from a Windows 95 start-up disk, those memory managers are probably not present (you'll need to find them on an existing Windows 95 or DOS 6.22 platform). If you try to execute the CONFIG.SYS file without those files present in their designated directories, the system will still boot, but it will return errors indicating that the specified files cannot be found. The last line is <Ctrl>+<Z>, which is an end-of-file character and saves the initial CONFIG.SYS file to your root directory. If you look at the root directory, you should see the CONFIG.SYS file listed. To review the contents of your CONFIG.SYS file at any point, type the following:

```
C:\> type config.sys  <Enter>
```

AUTOEXEC.BAT. The AUTOEXEC.BAT file is a batch file used to set system variables and start any necessary DOS Terminate and Stay Resident (TSR) Programs. Make sure you're in the C: drive root directory and then type

```
COPY CON AUTOEXEC.BAT  <Enter>
```

This opens a new file called AUTOEXEC.BAT. Now type the following:

```
PATH C:\DOS
```

```
prompt $p$g
^Z
```

The last line is <Ctrl>+<Z>, which is an end-of-file character and saves the initial AUTOEXEC.BAT file to your root directory. If you look at the root directory, you should see the AUTOEXEC.BAT file listed. To review the contents of your AUTOEXEC.BAT file at any point, type the following:

```
C:\> type autoexec.bat  <Enter>
```

> **NOTE:** The COPY CON trick can be handy in a pinch, but it's usually more convenient to use the EDIT or NOTEPAD utilities (or any other basic text editor) to create and edit your start-up files. However, you will be unable to use mouse functions with any of those utilities until you install the mouse in Step 11.

Testing the start-up files.   If you remove the floppy disk and reboot the system, you will notice that the system now boots directly to the C:> prompt *without* asking for the date and time. You'll also notice that as you change directories (i.e., cd dos), the prompt now indicates the current directory such as

```
C:\DOS\>_
```

This is because of the pg string included in your new AUTOEXEC.BAT file. Ideally, the start-up files should execute without any errors at all—the only two real issues are the presence of HIMEM.SYS and EMM386.EXE. As you add more devices to your system, you'll be making additions to your CONFIG.SYS and AUTOEXEC.BAT files.

REMarking start-up files.   From time to time, you're going to have problems with your start-up files—certain files may conflict or cause system problems, and you'll need to disable (or track down) offending com-

mand lines to straighten the problem out. You can simply delete a command line, but once the line is deleted,
it can be difficult (sometimes *very* difficult) to recreate
the command line. Instead, you can use the REM prefix to disable a command line in CONFIG.SYS or
AUTOEXEC.BAT. This stops the command line from
being processed but does not delete it. So if you find
you really need it later, you can just remove the REM
prefix to reenable the command line. Go ahead and
give it a try. Use the EDIT utility and load the CON-
FIG.SYS file and then REM-out the HIMEM,
EMM386, and DOS command lines:

```
REM device = c:\dos\himem.sys
REM device = C:\dos\emm386.exe ram
REM dos = umb,high
FILES = 50
BUFFERS = 20
^Z
```

Now save the changes, quit EDIT, and reboot. You'll
find that the REMed command lines are displayed but
not executed. If you plan to use Windows 95 exclusively, you can leave these lines REMmed-out. Otherwise, reedit the CONFIG.SYS file and remove the
REM statements (remember to save your changes).

Setting Up the Mouse

The mouse has become an indispensable part of
today's PC. Although DOS makes little use of the
mouse, many DOS programs can, and Windows 95
makes extensive use of the mouse. Now that the hard
drive and your start-up files are working, let's install
the mouse.

Step 11: Install the mouse

Let's get the mouse installed next. It's probably one of
the simplest installations that you'll ever accomplish.

PS/2 or serial connection.   If you have an open serial port, you can use a serial mouse. If your system has a PS/2-type mouse connector, choose a PS/2 mouse instead. The driver software is basically the same. Just attach the cable to the proper connector and you're on your way. Because mice are all serial devices, you should be able to buy an adapter that will convert a serial mouse to a PS/2 port (and vice versa).

Bus mouse.   The bus mouse is also a serial device, but it requires the use of a stand-alone adapter card to provide the interface. You'll need to configure the bus card properly and then install it into an open ISA slot. After you secure the bus card into place, you can attach the bus mouse.

> **NOTE:** Do not attempt to convert serial or PS/2 mice for use with a bus mouse card—they are incompatible.

Driver software.   Insert the mouse driver disk that came with your mouse and install the DOS mouse driver. Today, most DOS mouse drivers will install to their own directory on the hard drive and add a new command line to your CONFIG.SYS file (a few might add a line to AUTOEXEC.BAT instead). Run the driver's installation procedure and then check the CONFIG.SYS and AUTOEXEC.BAT files to see where the mouse driver has been installed:

```
C:\> type config.sys  <Enter>
C:\> type autoexec.bat  <Enter>
```

You'll probably find an entry such as the following in AUTOEXEC.BAT:

```
loadhigh c:\mouse.exe
```

Test the mouse.   Once the DOS driver is installed, reboot the computer. You should see a banner for the mouse driver when it is executed each time the computer starts. Next, switch to the DOS directory and start the EDIT utility:

```
C:\DOS> edit  <Enter>
```

After EDIT starts, move the mouse around. You will see the text mouse cursor moving around the screen— great job. For all practical purposes, this is all the testing you need to do.

Upgrading a mouse.   Exchanging one mouse for another one is simple enough to do, but the drivers can be a problem. Remember, if you install a different mouse, you'll probably need a different driver (especially under Windows 95). Install the new mouse drivers, edit your start-up file(s), and REM out any references to the old mouse. Remember to save your changes and reboot the PC for your changes to take effect.

Dealing with a troublesome mouse.   There are very few problems when installing a mouse. The most common problems in a new construction occur when the mouse driver fails to install or does not detect the mouse. If the mouse continues to be a problem, just follow the suggestions below:

- Check the mouse connector.

- Make sure the proper driver is installed (and that any command line switches are correct).

- Check for resource conflicts that might be interfering with the mouse.

- Clean the mouse.

- Replace the mouse.

Symptom 1: Mouse is not detected.   The mouse driver has probably failed to load because it could not detect the mouse hardware. In most cases, the mouse is not connected properly, or you put the serial connector on the wrong COM port. If everything is connected properly, the mouse may be defective.

Symptom 2: Mouse stalls or hesitates when moved. This is a common problem after you've been using the mouse for a while. In most cases, the mouse is dirty. Open the mouse, remove the mouse ball, and clean the ball with some light ammonia-based cleaner like Windex. A little ammonia in water will also work. Take a clean cotton swab and wipe the rollers inside the mouse. Replace the mouse ball and secure it. That should keep you going. If cleaning doesn't work, the mouse is not connected securely, the internal wiring is defective, or another device in the system is conflicting with the mouse's COM port.

Setting Up for Multimedia

Sound and images now play a vital role in games, presentations, and a great deal of business software. In order to handle such multimedia, you'll need to add sound support, as well as a CD-ROM drive. We'll end the section by wrapping up your hardware assembly.

Step 12: Assemble the sound system

Time for the fun stuff. Let's get the sound board installed next. Sound boards can be particularly troublesome because most sound boards use several different interrupts, I/O addresses, and at least one Direct Memory Access (DMA) channel. Most problems occur with hardware conflicts between the sound board and other devices in the system.

Configuring the sound board. Many of the newest sound boards use PnP technology to configure the board automatically. In that case, you'll need to install a DOS PnP manager to run the sound board under DOS and allow Windows 95 to identify the sound board when you install Windows 95 later. Traditional sound boards continue to use jumper settings for configuration—you'll need to set each jumper properly. Table 3.5 shows the settings for a typical Sound Blaster type of sound board.

Sound settings. Your sound circuit—the circuit that plays such sounds as .WAV files—requires an IRQ (usually IRQ 5), an I/O address (usually 220h or hexadecimal), and a DMA channel (usually DMA 1). Although the DMA channel and I/O address are rarely used by other devices, IRQ 5 is typically used by LPT2. If you only have one Line Printer Terminal (LPT) port in the system (LPT 1), it operates at IRQ 7, so using IRQ 5 for the sound board often works. If you have two LPT ports in the system, LPT 2 probably uses IRQ 5, so if you set the sound board to IRQ 5, you're going to have a hardware conflict. More advanced sound boards also offer address settings for a Frequency Modulation (FM) synthesizer and Wave Synthesizer.

CD settings. Chances are that your sound board has an interface for the CD-ROM (it doesn't matter right now whether the interface is ATAPI IDE or propri-

TABLE 3.5 Typical Configuration Settings for Sound Blaster 16 Pro

Jumper	Setting*
Interrupt (IRQ)	2, [5], 7, 10
8-bit DMA channel	0, [1], 3
16-bit DMA channel	[5], 6, 7
Audio I/O address	[220h], 240h, 260h, 280h
MIDI I/O address	300h, [330h]
Joystick I/O address	200h
FM synthesizer I/O address	388h
Wave synthesizer I/O address	N/A
IDE interface port	Secondary, [tertiary], quaternary
IDE interface IRQ	10, [11], 12, 14, 15

*Numbers in brackets are the default settings.

etary). If it does, there is probably another set of jumpers for the interface IRQ and I/O address. Remember that the CD-ROM interface—even though it's on the same board—is *totally* separate from the sound circuit. So it's possible that you may have a conflict with the sound function, but the CD-ROM works (or vice versa). Refer to the manual for your sound board and be sure to set the CD-ROM interface properly. If you're going to connect your ATAPI IDE CD-ROM to your existing drive controller, be sure to *disable* the sound board's CD-ROM interface.

MIDI settings.   Virtually all sound boards provide a MIDI channel. MIDI provides the orchestral-quality music that we have all become so accustomed to in such applications as PC games (like Master of Orion II or Emperor of the Fading Suns). The MIDI channel is easier to configure because it only requires an I/O channel (typically 330h) and can be set by a single jumper.

Game port settings.   If you look at the back of most Creative Labs (and many clone) sound boards, you'll see a 15-pin D-type connector. This connector serves two purposes: It allows for the connection of a MIDI device (such as a MIDI keyboard), and it can be used as a joystick port. There is usually a jumper on the sound board to select the port's function. The joystick port itself is almost always fixed at 200h or 201h. Remember, if there is another game port controller in the system, you should leave the sound board's game port *disabled*.

Installing the sound board.   There's no trick to installing a sound board (make sure the power is off and the PC is unplugged first). Simply set any on-board jumpers as needed, place the board into an available expansion slot (typically an ISA slot), and make sure that the board is seated properly. Secure the board's bracket with a screw. One thing that you should check is that the on-board volume control is set between 50 and 75 percent. If the card's volume is set low, the speakers will not produce the right volume, and you'll probably hear a lot of amplifier noise from the speakers because the speaker volume will have to be turned way up. Next, install your speakers. In most cases, this involves connecting the speakers with a 1/8-in stereo jack. If the speakers are powered externally, plug in the speakers now. If the speakers are battery powered, make sure that the batteries are fresh.

Plug-and-Play notes.   Over the last few years, sound boards have moved away from jumpers in favor of PnP technology. With Windows 95 and a PnP-compatible BIOS, the PnP sound board can literally configure itself each time the system initializes. To use a PnP sound board, you will need a system with Windows 95 and a PnP BIOS. If you have a slightly older motherboard, you may be able to upgrade the BIOS to a version that supports PnP.

Remember that a full PnP system will *only* work under Windows 95—when running under DOS or older versions of Windows, you'll need to add a DOS PnP driver [often called the Independent Configuration Utility (ICU)] under CONFIG.SYS. The driver disk that comes with your sound board probably contains the DOS PnP driver, and you'll need to install it along with your sound drivers and utilities.

Installing the sound software.   You probably noticed a driver disk enclosed with the sound board. This disk includes the drivers for DOS and Windows. Because you're still working under DOS, boot the system, place the disk in the floppy drive, and run the installation routine that will place the DOS drivers on your hard drive. The installation routine will add one or more command lines to your CONFIG.SYS—usually to add the DOS PnP manager. An example follows:

```
devicehigh = c:\plugplay\drivers\dos\dwcfgmg.sys
```

The installation routine will amend your AUTOEX-EC.BAT file to call the sound board's initialization routine and set system variables:

```
SET BLASTER = A220 IXX DX T1
SET SNDSCAPE = C:\SNDSCAPE
LH C:\SNDSCAPE\SSINIT /I
```

During the installation process, other sound utilities will be added, such as a test routine, sound recorder, and mixer. After the installation is complete, remove the disk and keep it aside for later—you'll need the protected-mode drivers for Windows 95. Reboot the system so that your changes will take effect. When the system reboots, you should see a banner indicating that the sound driver(s) have found the hardware and installed properly.

> **NOTE:** Most sound software also includes a basic test program which will play simple .WAV and MIDI files. Be sure to run any such test utility to verify the sound board before proceeding.

Upgrading the sound system.   Upgrading sound board hardware is usually a simple matter of replacing the sound board and reconnecting cables, but the sound drivers can be another matter. When a new sound board is installed, you're going to have to install the new sound drivers and disable the old ones. New drivers are often installed automatically using the software's installation routine, but you'll need to disable the old sound board's real-mode drivers in CON-FIG.SYS and AUTOEXEC.BAT (you can edit the start-up files through the DOS EDIT utility). Under Windows 95, the system will either autodetect a new PnP sound board (and proceed to update the protected-mode drivers), or you'll need to run the *Add New Hardware* wizard to identify the new hardware.

Dealing with a troublesome sound board.   Sound board installations are not always as smooth and simple as we would like to think—even for PnP systems. When trouble arises, be sure to check the following points:

- Double-check any configuration jumpers on the sound board.
- Eliminate any hardware conflicts.
- Check that the sound board is seated evenly and completely.
- Make sure that the sound volume is turned up.
- See that the sound drivers are properly installed.
- Make sure that the levels in your "mixer applet" are set adequately.
- See that the speakers are turned on and connected securely (also check the speaker volume).
- Replace the sound card.

Symptom 1: Drivers do not find the sound hardware. When the system powers up, you probably find an error message when the sound driver(s) attempt to load. In virtually all cases, the sound board is not configured properly, or the command line switches for your driver(s) do not match the hardware settings on the card. Check your hardware settings—make sure that the sound hardware does not conflict with other devices in the system. See that the appropriate command line switches match your hardware settings.

Symptom 2: No sound. There are lots of reasons for this. See that the speakers are connected to the Sound Output jack on your sound board. Turn the sound board volume up. Make sure the speakers are turned on. Finally, see that your sound software has installed completely (you may need to add an initialization utility to the AUTOEXEC.BAT file to start up the sound card under DOS).

Symptom 3: IDE drive problems. This can happen if your sound board's IDE port is using the same resources as

your system's secondary IDE port (on the motherboard or drive controller). If you have another suitable
drive controller in use, make sure to *disable* the sound
card's drive controller or configure the sound board as
a *tertiary* controller.

Step 13: Assemble the CD-
ROM drive system

Next, we're going to install the CD-ROM drive. For
the purposes of this section, we'll assume you're using
an ATAPI IDE CD-ROM drive, which could be
installed to the secondary channel of your EIDE controller *or* to the ATAPI IDE interface of a sound board.
Remember, if your sound board uses a *proprietary*
interface (there *are* 40-pin interfaces on some sound
boards that are *not* IDE—check it), you can only use
certain CD-ROM drives fitted with the *same* proprietary interface. On the other hand, an IDE CD-ROM
can be used with *any* IDE drive controller.

Choosing an interface.   Now you've got that IDE CD-
ROM, and you need to choose just where to install it.
As you saw above, you can use the secondary IDE
channel on your motherboard or drive controller board
or use the IDE interface on your sound board. Here
are some rules to help you choose the right course:

- If your sound board does *not* have a CD-ROM interface, it's an easy choice—just use the secondary
  IDE channel on your motherboard or drive controller board.

- If your sound board uses a proprietary interface,
  and the CD-ROM uses the same proprietary interface (you probably purchased the sound board and
  CD-ROM drive as a multimedia kit), *disable* the
  secondary IDE interface on your motherboard or
  drive controller board (unless there's already an
  IDE hard drive attached there) and use the sound
  board. As an alternative, you can leave the sec-

ondary IDE interface enabled and configure the sound card's drive interface as a *tertiary* controller.

- If it's an even choice between your IDE sound board interface and secondary IDE interface, use the secondary IDE interface on your motherboard or drive controller board. Be sure to *disable* the interface on your sound board.

> **NOTE:** If you're using an SCSI CD-ROM drive, the rules above do not apply—leave the secondary IDE interface as it is and disable the sound card's interface; then connect the SCSI CD-ROM to the SCSI chain and terminate as recommended.

Installing the IDE CD-ROM drive. Turn the system power off and unplug the AC line cord. Take a 40-pin IDE drive cable and locate the controller end (the connector that is by itself at one end). Plug the controller end of the cable into the drive controller. Be sure that the red side of the cable is oriented to the side of the header marked 1/2. If the CD-ROM drive is IDE, it probably has *primary* (master), *secondary* (slave), and *cable select* (CS) jumpers to define its position in the IDE channel. Chances are that the CD-ROM drive will be the only one on the channel. If so, set the CD-ROM drive to *primary* (master). Avoid using the cable select option unless the directions accompanying your CD-ROM specifically recommend it.

Next, select an available external drive bay, and slide the drive into place (you may need to add drive rails). Bolt the drive into place using four screws (using fewer than four may allow the drive to vibrate and fail prematurely). Connect the other end of the IDE cable to the 40-pin signal header on your CD-ROM drive. Be sure that the red side of the cable is oriented to the side of the header marked 1/2. Choose a four-pin power connector and plug it into the CD-ROM drive. Make sure the power connector is secure.

Finally, connect a slender four-wire CD audio cable between the four-pin audio connector on your CD-

ROM to the four-pin audio connector on your sound
board (usually located in the top middle portion of the
sound board). This cable allows you to play CD audio
directly through your sound board.

SCSI CD-ROM installation.   Installing an SCSI CD-
ROM drive is virtually identical to installing an IDE
CD-ROM. Turn the system power off and unplug the
AC line cord. Take a 50- or 68-pin SCSI cable and
locate an available drive connector. Chances are that
the cable is already attached to an SCSI controller
and hard drive. If not, connect one end of an SCSI
cable to the SCSI controller. Be sure that the red side
of the cable is oriented to the side of the header
marked 1/2. An SCSI CD-ROM will have several possible SCSI IDs available, so select an unused SCSI ID
via a jumper on the drive.

Next, select an available external drive bay, and
slide the drive into place (you may need to add drive
rails). Bolt the drive into place using four screws
(using fewer than four may allow the drive to vibrate
and fail prematurely). Connect the 50- or 68-pin SCSI
signal cable to the CD-ROM drive. Be sure that the
red side of the cable is oriented to the side of the header marked 1/2. You may need to reterminate the SCSI
chain to ensure that only the end-most devices are
terminated. Choose a four-pin power connector and
plug it into the CD-ROM drive. Make sure the power
connector is secure.

Finally, connect a slender four-wire CD audio cable
between the four-pin audio connector on your CD-
ROM to the four-pin audio connector on your sound
board (usually located in the top middle portion of the
sound board). This cable allows you to play CD audio
directly through your sound board.

Installing the CD-ROM software.   When you first restart
the system after the CD-ROM hardware is installed,
the system will *not* recognize the CD-ROM drive. CD-

ROM drives require two pieces of software under DOS: a low-level driver and a DOS extension for assigning the drive letter. The driver disk that accompanies your CD-ROM drive usually has an installation routine that will place the driver files on the hard drive and make the necessary additions to your CONFIG.SYS and AUTOEXEC.BAT files.

Low-level driver. The low-level driver is a critically important piece of software because it allows the PC to talk directly with the CD hardware. ATAPI drivers allow the IDE interface to communicate with the CD-ROM, but you will need the ATAPI driver that is *specific* to the particular CD-ROM drive. If you do not have a driver disk, you can usually download the ATAPI driver from the web site of your particular CD-ROM drive manufacturer. The low-level driver is installed in your CONFIG.SYS file as

```
devicehigh = c:\cdd\wcd.sys /D:wp_cdrom
```

SCSI driver installation is very similar. A low-level real-mode driver will be needed in order to run the SCSI CD-ROM drive under DOS. In actual practice, you'll see a command line in CONFIG.SYS such as

```
device = c:\scsi\neccdr.sys /D:neccd
REM the lastdrive statement is not viral, but
included to allow the REM reassignment of drive
letters
lastdrive = z
```

MSCDEX. This is the classic CD-ROM DOS extension that allows DOS to interact with a CD-ROM by specifying file systems, assigning drive letters, and so on. MSCDEX is usually installed along with your low-level driver. If you don't have MSCDEX (or need to update an older version), you can download it from the Microsoft web site (http://www.microsoft.com/kb/articles/q123/4/08.htm). MSCDEX is placed in the AUTOEXEC.BAT file as follows:

```
lh c:\cdd\mscdex.exe /D:wp_cdrom /M:20
```

SCSI installations also require the use of MSCDEX. The command line will be very similar:

```
REM this will configure the SCSI CD-ROM under DOS
as drive "L"
c:\scsi\mscdex /D:neccd /L:L
```

Testing the CD-ROM drive. After your software is installed, reboot the system. You should see the banners for your low-level driver and MSCDEX. These normally indicate that the interface and CD-ROM drive have been found and are responding properly. Let's run a few quick tests to see if the drive is working.

CD audio. Place that favorite Tony Bennett audio CD in the drive and try playing it. Chances are that your sound board software package installed a CD player applet. Start the CD player and play a track or two. Of course, you'll need a sound board with speakers, as well as a CD audio cable attached between the CD-ROM and sound board.

CD data. Place a data CD in the drive, switch to the CD-ROM drive letter (i.e., D: or E:), and check the directory for a file list. After a moment, the directory should appear. This should confirm that the drive is working. If you get an error such as "Error reading from drive D:," the disc may need a moment to initialize after it is placed in the drive—try reinserting the disc.

Dealing with a troublesome CD-ROM drive. As with most other areas of the PC, CD-ROM drive installations do not always proceed as easily as you would like. For problems with new installations, start by checking the issues below:

- Check that the CD-ROM interface signal cable is attached properly.

- Make sure that the CD-ROM does not coexist on the same channel with a hard drive.

- Check the CD audio cable between the CD-ROM and sound board.

- Make sure that the power connector is installed correctly.

- Check the CD-ROM drive assignment jumper(s).

- See that a valid readable CD is installed in the drive.

- Check the low-level driver installation, verify the command line switches, and check for the latest version.

- Check the MSCDEX installation, verify the command line switches (see that they match the low-level driver switches), and check for the latest version.

- Replace the CD-ROM drive.

Symptom 1: The drive fails to spin up. You power up the system, but you do not hear the drive motor or see the drive light. There is also probably a drive error when the low-level driver attempts to load (the CD-ROM drive hardware cannot be found). In virtually all cases, you forgot to plug in the power connector, or the connector is not secured properly. If problems persist, the drive is probably defective.

Symptom 2: The drivers fail to load. The main reasons your low-level driver and/or MSCDEX may fail to load are because (1) the interface or hard drive is not configured properly (or is conflicting with other hardware in the system) or (2) the command line switches in your low-level driver or MSCDEX do not match the hardware settings. Also verify that the drive is powered properly, and the drive jumpers are configured correctly.

Symptom 3: No CD audio. If you cannot hear CD audio, make sure that your speakers are on and the sound card volume is turned up properly. Also make sure that the CD audio cable is attached properly between the CD-ROM drive and the sound board. Try listening to the audio through a set of headphones plugged into the speaker jack on the CD. If the headphone works but the audio does not play through the sound board, the audio cable is not attached or defective.

Another possibility is that the CD Input in your sound board's mixer applet is set low. Most current sound boards incorporate a mixer applet as part of their normal operation. The mixer tells the sound board how to treat the various inputs (i.e., .WAV, mic input, CD audio) that it may receive. If the CD audio input is set too low, you won't hear it. Start the DOS mixer applet and adjust the CD audio setting.

Step 14: Wrapping up the initial hardware

By now, your new PC is basically complete and tested, and you're ready to start closing things up. There may be other supplemental pieces of hardware to install (such as a modem or DVD-ROM drive), but now is the time to install your operating system. Before you rush on to Sec. 4, take some time to make the following sanity checks below:

System precautions.   Don't close up the system just yet, you need to perform a few last-minute checks first:

Snug the bolts.   Examine each screw you installed on the motherboard, expansion boards, and drives. Make sure that each screw is secure (they should be snug but not overtightened). Loose screws can eventually work free from the vibrations inside the PC and may fall out—sometimes into live circuitry.

Check the cards.   Each expansion card should be seated properly and completely in its bus slot. The

card (especially full-length cards) should not interfere with the CPU, SIMMs, or any other device on
the motherboard.

Routing cables.   Check the way each of your ribbon
cables is routed through the case. Keep the cables
away from known sources of electrical noise, such as
power supplies, fans, and video cards.

Back up the CMOS.   Once you have the system
CMOS settings optimized just the way you want,
take a <PrnScr> of each "page." This prints out the
data for you (and eliminates a lot of writing). Keep
the pages with your system manuals.

Burn-in policy.   The rule for reliability in electronic
equipment is that a device will either fail promptly or
will work for a long time (well, at least until it's out of
warranty). With this in mind, you should burn in the
PC for several days and test it periodically throughout
that time to see that everything is still working. The
idea is that if something fails *right away,* you can
exchange it. For individual PC builders, burn-in periods are often considered somewhat optional. However,
professional PC builders should *seriously* consider
running a burn-in period for *every* new machine they
build.

> **NOTE:** The burn-in policy is simply a quality control
> measure. Omitting a burn-in period will certainly not
> harm a new PC, but you may not catch problem compo-
> nents that might fail in the field later.

Button up the system.   If you're done with new hardware installations, bolt the outer cover into place
(watch out for those sharp metal edges). If you still
have other hardware to install, leave the cover off for
now while we install the operating system.

Installing the Operating System

Even though the basic hardware construction of your new PC is complete, you're still not quite done. Your new system needs an *operating system*—for this book, we'll be installing the CD version of Microsoft's Windows 95. If you require a different operating system, such as Linux, OS/2, or Windows NT, you should refer to the specific installation procedures for that particular OS. Once the operating system is installed, we'll cover some additional installation procedures for modems, a second hard drive, a DVD-ROM drive (and MPEG decoder card), and a joystick. You'll also see a generic procedure for upgrading a BIOS ROM.

Installing Windows 95

Now that you have your CD-ROM and mouse installed, you're ready to install Windows 95. We won't go through the entire step-by-step installation process because Microsoft has already provided extensive instructions with the Windows 95 package (Windows 95 also provides a comprehensive Setup

Wizard), but now is a good time to cover some of the important points to remember before dropping that Windows 95 CD into the system.

Step 15: Getting ready for the installation

Most of the problems associated with a Windows 95 installation are due to a lack of preparation. The hardware is incomplete, improperly installed, or the CMOS is set incorrectly. Before you attempt to install (or reinstall) Windows 95, take some time to review the following suggestions.

Prove out the hardware.   Windows 95 is extremely adept at identifying hardware and adapting itself accordingly. However, hardware faults or conflicts can easily confuse the Setup utility and halt the installation. Be sure to resolve any hardware conflicts or replace any defective devices. Always make sure that your hardware works under DOS *first*—before beginning your Windows 95 installation.

Disable BIOS virus checking.   Many modern BIOS versions include a boot sector virus checker (Fig. 4.1) that

Boot Options

First Boot Device	Floppy	**F1**	Help
Second Boot Device	Hard Disk	**ESC**	Back
Third Boot Device	Disabled	**Enter**	Select
Fourth Boot Device	Disabled		
		>	Previous Item
System Cache	Enabled	**>**	Next Item
Boot Speed	Turbo	**>**	Select Menu
Num Lock	Off		
		F5	Setup Defaults
Boot Sector Protection	Enabled	**F6**	Previous Values
		F10	Save & Exit
Typematic Rate Programming	Default		

Figure 4.1   Disabling the Boot Sector Virus Checker in CMOS.

prevents any changes from being made to the HDD's boot sector, but Windows 95 will *need* to make changes to the boot sector so that Windows 95 will load. This usually causes false virus errors during installation. Before starting the installation, go into your CMOS Setup and disable the boot sector protection option.

Identify your hardware. Make sure you have a complete list of the hardware in your system. Windows 95 is pretty good at identifying PC hardware automatically, but with all the different types of hardware in the market (especially those that came *after* the release of Windows 95), you may need to identify hardware specifically. You don't want to be fishing for that information at the last minute. It would also be helpful to have any of those Windows 95 driver disks you've been putting aside during your system assembly in Secs. 2 and 3.

Check for viruses. Ideally, you own a good virus checker like Norton Anti-Virus (www.symantec.com) or McAfee's VirusScan (www.mcafee.com). Do a complete scan for viruses now. Remember to check for viruses on *all* of your disks, as well as in memory. In actual practice, your new system has an absolute minimum of files, so the chances of a virus are pretty small, but you should still perform a check to be certain.

Prepare the HDD. Windows is not very forgiving of hard drive problems such as cross-linked files and lost allocation units (or clusters). Run ScanDisk to check for any drive problems (you can run ScanDisk from your bootable disk if it's not already on the hard drive). Correct any file problems and then run Defrag to defragment the drive (also available on the bootable disk). If the drive is new, you probably don't need to worry about the drive's condition, but try it anyway. The practice will do you good.

Backup the HDD.   Now is the time to back up your PC. Of course, if this is a new build, there is probably nothing on the hard drive that needs to be backed up, but if you're upgrading an existing Windows 3.1x system, it's a good idea to perform a complete system backup to tape or removable media drive (Zip, Jaz, SyJet, and so on) before proceeding with a Windows 95 installation.

Have protected-mode driver disks ready.   Windows 95 is going to use protected-mode (32-bit) drivers for almost everything in your PC. The Windows 95 CD contains a lot of 32-bit drivers for your hardware already, but if you have any unusual or late-model hardware (such as a top-end video board made after August of 1995), you should have the disks with Windows 95 drivers handy. If you put your driver disks aside while going through Secs. 2 and 3, gather them together now.

Simplify your start-up files.   Finally, some TSRs and real-mode device drivers may interfere with Windows 95 Setup, so take a look at your CONFIG.SYS and AUTOEXEC.BAT files and disable any drivers or TSRs other than those used for your mouse, CD-ROM, and sound board. Some memory managers like 386MAX may also cause problems, so disable your memory manager, too.

Start the Setup prodecure.   Reboot your system (if you needed to make any changes to your start-up files), drop in the Windows 95 CD, and begin the Setup process to install Windows 95. The Setup Wizard will guide you through all of the steps needed to complete the installation successfully.

Step 16: Make a start-up disk

Once the Windows 95 Setup is complete, make a Windows 95 start-up disk for your own system (the step-by-step process is outlined under the heading "Boot Disk" of Sec. 2). Mark the disk clearly and put it aside, preferably with the documentation for your system. If you have trouble starting Windows 95, that start-up disk may be your only way out.

> **NOTE:** Make sure to create a new start-up disk each time you make a major change to your system.

Step 17: Dealing with installation and backup problems

Ideally, your Windows 95 installation went flawlessly, and you've now got Windows 95 booting successfully on your new system. Unfortunately, not all installations are perfect, and there are many problems that can plague the Setup process. The following outline some of the most common symptoms and solutions encountered when installing or upgrading to Windows 95. If your installation went smoothly, feel free to skip directly to Step 17.

Symptom 1: The Windows 95 boot drive is no longer bootable after restoring data with the DOS backup utility.
This happens frequently when a replacement drive is installed, and you attempt to restore the Windows 95 backup data. Unfortunately, the DOS version of Backup is not configured to restore system files. Start Backup and restore your root directory with *System Files, Hidden Files,* and *Read Only Files* checked. Next, boot the system from an MS-DOS 6.x upgrade setup disk #1 or a Windows 95 start-up disk and then use the SYS command to make the hard drive bootable:

```
A:\> sys c:  <Enter>
```

You should then be able to restore the remainder of your files.

When backing up a Windows 95 system, your best approach is to use the Windows 95 Backup program. Once the new drive is installed, partitioned, and formatted, install a new copy of Windows 95, start Windows 95 Backup, and *then* restore the remaining files to the drive.

> **NOTE:** When replacing an operational hard drive with a new (usually larger) one, you can use the Drive Copy utility from PowerQuest (www.powerquest.com) to transfer the original files to your new drive without the hassle of traditional backups and restores.

Symptom 2: Windows 95 will not boot, and ScanDisk reports bad clusters that it cannot repair. This is a problem frequently encountered with Western Digital hard drives. If your WD drive fails in this way, you can recover the drive, but you will lose all the information on it. Back up as much information from the drive as possible before proceeding:

- Download the Western Digital service files WDATIDE.EXE and WD_CLEAR.EXE from www.wdc.com. You can also get these files from AOL by typing keyword WDC.

- Copy these files to a clean boot floppy disk.

- Boot to DOS from a clean disk (no CONFIG.SYS or AUTOEXEC.BAT files) and run WD_CLEAR.EXE. This utility clears all data on the media (and destroys all data).

- Next, run the WDATIDE.EXE utility to perform a comprehensive surface scan.

- Repartition and reformat the drive and then restore your data.

> **NOTE:** If your hard drive is not a Western Digital drive, check with the particular drive manufacturer for similar corrective actions. Do *not* use the files mentioned above on any other drive.

**Symptom 3: You see a "Bad or missing <filename>"
error message on start-up.**   A file used by Windows 95
during start-up has probably become corrupt. Locate
the file mentioned in the error message. Run Windows
95 Setup again and select the *Verify* option in Safe
Recovery to replace the missing or damaged file(s).
Otherwise, if you can find the file, erase it, and try
reinstalling it from original Windows 95 disks or CD.
If you cannot isolate the offending file, repartition and
reformat the drive and then reinstall Windows 95
from scratch.

**Symptom 4: Windows 95 reports damaged or missing core
files or a "VxD error" message.**   During start-up,
Windows 95 depends on several important Virtual
Driver (VxD) files being available. If a VxD file is
damaged or missing, Windows 95 will not function
properly (if it loads at all). Run Windows 95 Setup
again and select the *Verify* option in Safe Recovery to
replace the missing or damaged file(s).

**Symptom 5: After installing Windows 95, you can no
longer boot from a different hard drive.**   The Windows 95
Setup program checks all hard disks to find just *one*
that contains the 80h designator in the DriveNumber
field of a boot sector. Windows 95 will typically force
the first drive to be bootable and *prevent* other drives
from booting. However, there are two ways to correct
the problem after Windows 95 is installed. You can
use the version of FDISK included with Windows 95
to manually set the primary active partition or use a
disk editor utility to change a disk's DriveNumber
field so that you can boot from that particular hard
disk (the latter should be attempted *only* by experienced technicians).

Symptom 6: Windows 95 Registry files are missing.
There are two registry files: USER.DAT and SYS-
TEM.DAT. They are also backed up as USER.DA0 and

SYSTEM.DA0. If a .DAT file is missing, Windows 95
will automatically load the corresponding .DA0 file. If
both the .DAT and .DA0 Registry files are missing or
corrupt, Windows 95 will start in the Safe Mode offer-
ing to restore the Registry. However, this cannot be
accomplished without a backup. Either restore the
Registry files from a tape or disk backup or run
Windows 95 Setup to create a new Registry.
Unfortunately, restoring an old registry or creating a
new registry from scratch will force you to reload programs and reinstall hardware to restore the system to
its original state—a long and difficult procedure. In
the future, use the following DOS procedure to back
up the Registry files to a floppy disk:

```
attrib -r -s -h system.da?
attrib -r -s -h user.da?
copy system.da? A:\
copy user.da? A:\
attrib +r +s +h system.da?
attrib +r +s +h user.da?
```

**Symptom 7: During the Windows 95 boot process, there is
an "Invalid System Disk" error message.**   This often
happens during the first reboot during Windows 95
Setup or when you boot from the start-up disk. If you
see a message such as "Invalid system disk—replace
the disk, and then press any key," there are several
possible problems that can cause this type of error.
Check for viruses first. Your disk may be infected with
a boot-sector virus. Run your antivirus work disk and
check closely for boot sector viruses. Windows 95
Setup may fail if there is antivirus software running
as a TSR or your BIOS has enabled boot sector protection. Make sure that any boot sector protection is
turned off before installing Windows 95. Also,
Windows 95 may not successfully detect disk management software such as Disk Manager, EZ-Drive, or
DrivePro and may accidentally overwrite the Master
Boot Record (MBR). See the documentation that accom-

panies your particular management software for recovering the MBR. To reinstall the Windows 95 system files, follow the steps below:

- Boot the system using the Windows 95 Emergency Boot Disk.

- At the MS-DOS command prompt, type the following lines:

```
c:
cd\windows\command
attrib c:\msdos.sys -h -s -r
ren c:\msdos.sys c:\msdos.xxx
a:
sys c:
del c:\msdos.sys
ren c:\msdos.xxx c:\msdos.sys
attrib c:\msdos.sys +r +s +h
```

- Remove the Emergency Boot Disk and reboot the system.

Symptom 8: Windows 95 will not install on a compressed drive. You are probably using an old version of the compression software that Windows 95 does not recognize. Although Windows 95 should be compatible with all versions of SuperStor, it does require version 2.0 or later of Stacker. Make sure your compression software is recent, and see that there is enough free space on the host drive to support Windows 95 installation.

Symptom 9: The hard drive indicates that it is in the "MS-DOS compatibility mode." For some reason, Windows 95 is using a real-mode (DOS) driver instead of a protected-mode (32-bit) driver. Make sure that any software related to the hard drive (especially hard disk drivers) is using the protected-mode versions. Windows 95 should install equivalent protected-mode software, but you may need to contact the drive manufacturer and obtain the latest Windows 95 drivers. If you are using Disk Manager, make sure that you're using version 6.0 or later. You can get the latest patch (DMPATCH.EXE) from the Ontrack Web site (www.ontrack.com). Finally, Windows 95 may use DOS compatibility mode on large EIDE hard disks (hard disks with more than 1024 cylinders) in some computers. This may occur because of an invalid drive geometry translation in the system ROM BIOS that prevents the protected-mode IDE device driver from being loaded. Contact your system manufacturer for information about obtaining an updated BIOS.

Symptom 10: Disabling the protected-mode disk driver(s) hides the partition table when FDISK is used. As with Symptom 9, there are problems preventing 32-bit operation of your hard drive(s). Do *not* use the "Disable all 32-bit protected-mode disk drivers" option. Instead, upgrade your motherboard BIOS to a later version.

Step 18: Optimizing Windows 95

Because Windows 95 is generally quite good at detecting system hardware, it tries to configure itself to your system in an optimal fashion—that's dynamite in theory but not always so slick in actual practice. If you want to tweak your system optimizations, Windows 95 provides several means of optimizing your system manually.

Optimizing video. Video performance has always been a bottleneck for Windows platforms, and graphics adapters have come a long way to improve Windows performance. This is especially noticeable in higher resolutions and color depths where more data is needed to represent a full screen image. Windows 95 provides a dialog that allows you to adjust the amount of graphics acceleration for your system. As a rule, maximum graphics acceleration is preferred, but high graphics acceleration may have an adverse effect on the system at some resolutions and color depths.

Once Windows is running, select *Start, Settings,* and *Control Panel* and then click on the *System* icon. Select the *Performance* tab, then click on the "Graphics" button. This brings up the *Advanced Graphics Settings* dialog (Fig. 4.2). You'll note the slider bar that controls the amount of hardware acceleration applied to the video system. If this slider is *already* at the maximum setting, leave it alone and just select *Cancel* to back out. If the slider is *not* at maximum, try increasing the amount of acceleration and see if that improves your overall system performance.

Optimizing the hard drive. Next to video, the hard drive has the most profound effect on your Windows 95 system performance. Hard drives are accessed *much* more slowly than RAM (orders of magnitude more slowly). Because Windows 95 (and its applications) make heavy use of the hard drive for data and virtual memory, slow file access and hardware will appear to slow down your Windows 95 system. You can optimize both the Windows 95 file system and virtual memory allocation to improve system performance.

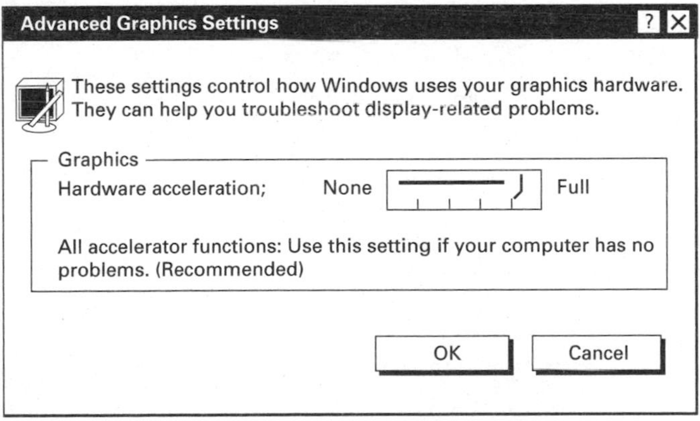

Figure 4.2 The *Advanced Graphics Settings* dialog.

Adjusting the file system. Once Windows is running, select *Start, Settings,* and *Control Panel* and then click on the *System* icon. Select the *Performance* tab and then click on the File System button. This brings up the *File System Properties* dialog (Fig. 4.3). There are two entries: a pull-down menu specifying the role of the machine and a slider that adjusts your drive caching (read-ahead optimization). Make sure that the entry in your pull-down menu accurately reflects the use of your PC (almost always a desktop). The caching slider is probably set to the maximum value. If not, try increasing the read-ahead optimization and see if you pick up any performance improvements there.

Adjusting the virtual memory. Virtual memory is the use of drive space to simulate the role of RAM. More specifically, segments of RAM are swapped onto and off of your hard drive. This allows you to run applications that would otherwise require more physical RAM than you have in your system. However, the reg-

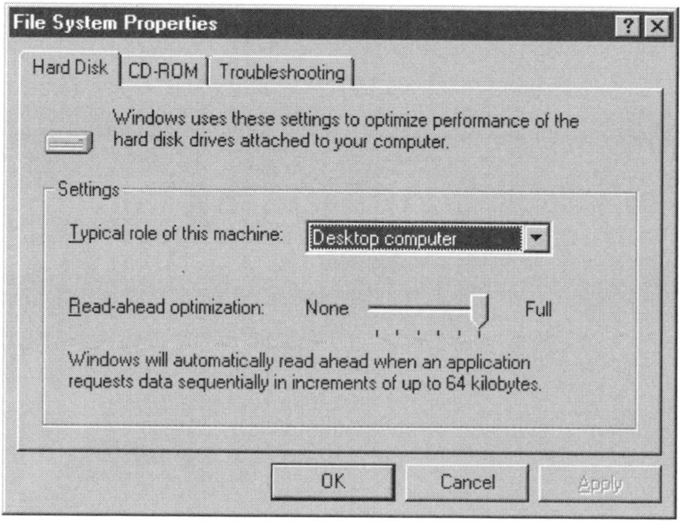

Figure 4.3 The *File System Properties* dialog.

ular swapping of data to and from the drive *does* slow the system. Ideally, you would like to set the virtual memory to a size that is large enough to be useful but small enough to minimize swapping.

One of the improvements to Windows 95 is that not only will it determine the optimum swap file size, but the swap file size is dynamic—it can be grown or shrunk as needed. Normally, you do not need to tinker with virtual memory (just leave it on automatic). However, you should at least know to turn it off. Once Windows is running, select *Start, Settings,* and *Control Panel* and then click on the *System* icon. Select the *Performance* tab and then click on the Virtual Memory button. This brings up the *Virtual Memory* dialog (Fig. 4.4). Normally, most of the dialog is grayed-out and Windows 95 runs the swap file automatically. However, you can select to set your own swap file settings. If you select that option, you can also set the check box to *disable* virtual memory.

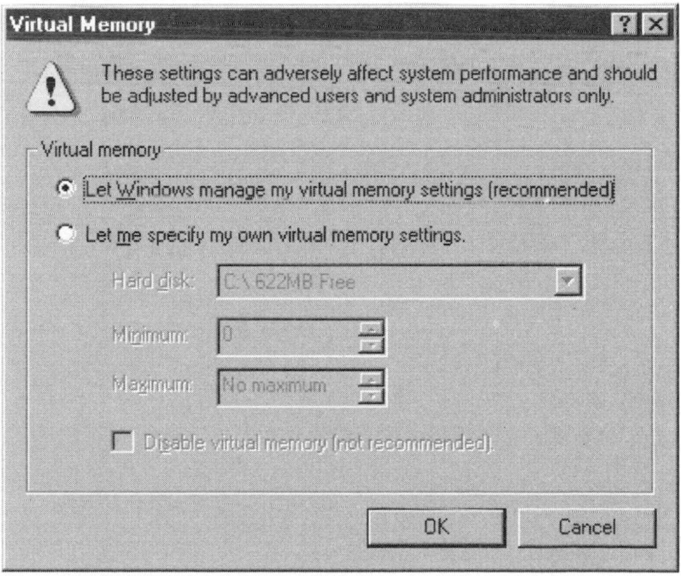

Figure 4.4 The *Virtual Memory* dialog.

NOTE: The ultimate means of virtual memory improvement would be to *minimize* the need for a swap file by adding more RAM to the system (usually above 32 to 64 Mbytes of RAM).

Optimizing the CD-ROM drive. The CD-ROM drive is far slower than the hard drive. Fortunately, it is accessed far less often than a hard drive. Even so, when a CD-ROM is used, its slow data transfer time can be a problem. Windows 95 helps to compensate for this by supporting built-in CD-ROM drive caching (caching with older utilities such as SmartDrive are eliminated). It is possible to optimize the CD-ROM caching for best performance.

Once Windows is running, select *Start, Settings,* and *Control Panel* and then click on the *System* icon. Select the *Performance* tab and then click on the File System button. This brings up the *File System Properties* dialog. Select the CD-ROM tab (Fig. 4.5). There are two entries, a slider controlling the amount of supplemental cache provided for the CD-ROM drive

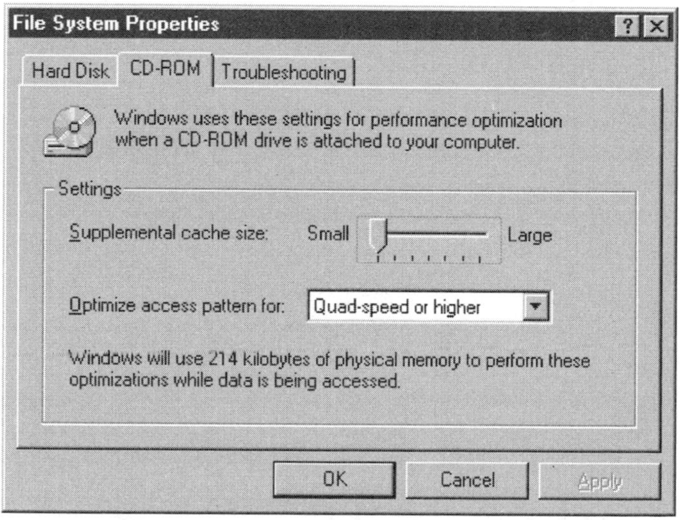

Figure 4.5   Optimizing the CD-ROM performance.

and a pull-down menu allowing you to optimize the CD-ROM access. If the supplemental cache slider is not at its maximum level, increase its value. You may not see any direct improvement until the CD-ROM is accessed. Make sure that the entry in your pull-down menu is set for your drive speed. In virtually all cases, the entry should be "Quad speed or higher."

Supplemental Installations

By now, your new PC should be essentially complete, with Windows 95 running properly. But for many PC users, there are some additional pieces of hardware that still must be added to the system. This part of the section highlights the more popular supplemental hardware installations. We've waited until now to discuss these installations because the hardware is either nonessential or relies heavily on Windows 95 resources for proper operation.

Step 19: Installing a modem

Of all the PC upgrades available, the hottest upgrade today has to be the modem. A modem allows two or more PCs to communicate and network over global distances using the public telephone system. Getting on-line with AOL and the Internet has certainly become the "thing to do," and fast modems are available at relatively low prices. Most full-featured modems work under DOS, but virtually all on-line access software for services like CompuServe, AOL, and the Internet are Windows-based.

Modem drivers.   One thing to remember about *all* modems is that they can be *extremely* finicky to set up—they demand a driver that is *specific* to that *exact* modem make and model. The driver disk that accompanies your modem probably has a protected-mode driver for Windows 95. If not, download it from the manufacturer's Web site *before* starting your modem installation.

If you do *not* have the specific driver for your exact modem (this often happens with second-hand or hand-me-down modems), you *may* be able to use a generic driver, such as a Hayes generic driver, but generic drivers don't always work and almost always limit the features that are available from the modem. If you *must* use an alternative driver, get the proper driver installed.

Installing an external modem.   An external modem is a self-contained device that uses one of your PC's COM ports (i.e., COM1 or COM2). If you have a mouse plugged into COM1, use COM2 for the modem (and vice versa). Remember that an external modem requires an external power source, so you'll need to have an extra AC outlet nearby for that power pack (and count on that power pack obstructing one or two other AC outlets).

The advantage of an external modem is that it is very "plug and play"—there are no jumpers to set. Just connect the external modem to the serial port, turn things on, and fire up Windows 95. Once Windows 95 starts, use the *Add New Hardware* wizard under the *Control Panel* to inform Windows 95 of your new installation. The driver disk that accompanies your external modem may even have an automated installation routine that will update Windows 95 for you.

The disadvantage to an external modem is that it can be limited by your COM port. This is certainly not a problem when using state-of-the-art motherboards with fast Universal Asychronous Receiver/Transmitters (UARTs), but sticking a fast modem on an older system may require you to disable the existing COM port(s) and install a multi-I/O board with high-speed COM ports available.

Installing an internal modem. Generally speaking, all internal modems demand an ISA port, so you will need to have one ISA port available before you pull the shrink wrap off that new box. Remember that internal modems already have complete COM port circuitry built-in, so you will have to configure the modem to use a specific COM port (i.e., COM1 or COM2) and then disable the corresponding COM port on your motherboard (or other multi-I/O card). Plug the modem into an available ISA slot and secure it into place.

The most frequent cause of internal modem installation problems is resource conflicts with existing COM ports or other devices in the system. For example, you often have resource conflicts if you configure the modem to use COM1 and there is already a COM1 port elsewhere in the system (even if there's no device attached to the COM port, the active ports themselves can cause problems). Table 4.1 illustrates the typical settings for COM1 through COM4. Modems require relatively little power, so installing a modem will very rarely overload a power supply (the system would have to be marginal to begin with). Also notice that COM ports tend to share interrupts. Specifically, COM1 and COM3 share IRQ4, and COM2 and COM4 share IRQ3. Even though each COM port uses a unique I/O address, having COM1/COM3 or COM2/COM4 in the same system can result in hardware conflicts.

Once Windows 95 starts, it normally checks for hardware. In many cases, Windows 95 will detect the

TABLE 4.1 IRQ and I/O Settings for COM1 Through COM4

COM port	IRQ	I/O address (hex)
COM1	4	3F8h
COM2	3	2F8h
COM3	4	3E8h
COM4	3	2E8h

new internal modem and attempt to install the drivers for it automatically. Given the trouble with modem drivers, do not allow Windows 95 to install its own drivers unless you're *absolutely* sure that Windows 95 will install the right driver for your specific modem. In most cases, you can let Windows 95 install the drivers from the driver disk accompanying the modem. If Windows 95 does not autodetect the internal modem, you can run the *Add New Hardware* wizard.

Step 20: Installing a second hard drive

It's odd that we never seem to have enough hard drive space. No matter how large the hard drives become, we always seem to have them filled in just a few months. Eventually, you may choose to install a second hard drive—the procedure is less stressful than trying to back up and restore files when replacing your primary hard drive.

Planning the location.   Before dropping more money into a second hard drive, give some thought to where you'll put it. Remember that your second hard drive will need a drive bay. This may pose a problem for baby and small desktop cases that already have a floppy drive, CD-ROM drive, and primary hard drive in place. Find an available drive bay and an unused four-pin power connector from the power supply.

Also consider the EIDE cable. Remember that a single cable can support two drives, but the drives have to be close enough together for the cable to reach. If your only other drive bay is on the other side of the case, you're going to have problems. Once you choose a drive bay, make sure the cable will reach. If it doesn't, you may also need to purchase a longer EIDE signal cable. The same idea holds true for SCSI signal cables.

Setting the jumpers.   Right now, there is a single drive on your primary EIDE channel set as the *primary* (or master) drive. First, set the new drive so that it is jumpered as the *secondary* (or slave) drive. Check the original drive to be sure that it is jumpered as the primary drive in a two-drive system—some drives make a distinction between being the primary drive in a single-drive system and in a two-drive system. Check the jumpers on your original drive to be sure. Do not jumper the drive as CS (or cable select). For SCSI hard drives, you'll need to configure the SCSI ID. The first SCSI hard drive is jumpered as ID 0, and a second hard drive should be jumpered as ID 1.

Installing the second drive. Slide the new drive into its drive bay and then secure the drive with four screws. Remember to use four screws to secure the drive evenly—fewer screws may allow the drive to vibrate and result in a premature failure. Also do not overtighten the screws. Too much force may warp the drive frame slightly and cause a premature failure.

Cabling the second drive. Attach the EIDE or SCSI signal cable to the new drive. Remember to align the red side of the cable (pin 1) with the side of the drive signal header marked 1/2. Unlike floppy drives, it does not matter which of the signal connectors attach to your primary or secondary drives. Next, attach the power cable to your new drive.

If you're installing an SCSI hard drive, you may also need to reterminate the SCSI chain—remember that an SCSI chain needs two (and only two) terminators. In most cases, the SCSI adapter is terminated, and the end-most device of the SCSI chain is terminated. If the second SCSI hard drive becomes the *last* device on the SCSI cable, you should move the terminators to that new hard drive.

Preparing the new drive. You should restart the system and enter the CMOS Setup. Enter the proper drive parameters in CMOS (or set the CMOS to autodetect the drive). Save your changes and reboot the system. If you've installed an SCSI hard drive, make sure that the CMOS entry for the drive is set to "none" or "not installed." Boot the system from your floppy disk and prepare the secondary drive as you did the original drive. Use FDISK to partition the new drive (you may create several partitions on the new drive) and then use FORMAT to prepare each new partition on the drive for DOS (Windows 95 will recognize it). You should then remove the boot disk and allow the system to boot normally.

Remember that adding a second hard drive can upset your drive letters on the original drive. DOS/Windows assigns drive letters to primary DOS partitions first and then to extended DOS partitions. So if you place a primary DOS partition on the new drive, the D: letter will shift from the second partition of the original drive to the primary partition of the new drive, and the original D: will become E:, and so on. The way to avoid this shifting of drive letters is to use only extended DOS partitions on the new drive.

> **NOTE:** There have been problems reported with the original release of FDISK for Windows 95 that can cause problems when creating more than one partition on the same physical drive. Use the real-mode version of FDISK with DOS 6.22 if possible.

> **NOTE:** Remember to be *extremely* careful when using FDISK and FORMAT to prepare a second drive. Do not accidentally repartition or reformat your original drive.

Reassigning the CD-ROM drive letter. The new hard drive will be assigned to at least one drive letter (more if there is more than one partition on the new drive). This will affect your CD-ROM drive because the new drive letter will almost certainly be the same as the CD-ROM. You will need to reassign the CD-ROM's drive letter. You can accomplish this under Windows 95 by selecting *Start, Settings, Control Panel,* and

System. Select the *Device Manager* tab and then high-light the *CD-ROM* entry. When you bring up the CD-ROM's properties, you can enter a new drive letter.

Under DOS, you will need to add the /L switch to your MSCDEX command line entry in AUTO-EXEC.BAT. This allows you to assign the CD-ROM drive to a new letter. For example, the switch /L:F will make the CD-ROM use the letter F:.

Reinstalling CD applications. Although reassigning a CD-ROM drive letter is an easy process, reassigning the drive letter for CD-ROM applications is not so easy. If you encounter a CD-based application that refuses to run after the CD-ROM drive letter is changed, you will need to reinstall that application.

Step 21: Installing a joystick

If you play games on your PC—especially flight simulators or driving programs—sooner or later you're going to need a joystick. There are many different features in today's joysticks, but they all perform the same basic functions and use the same kind of interface. As a result, joysticks are quick and simple to install.

Attaching a joystick. All joysticks use a game port interface provided through a 15-pin subminiature D-type connector. Game ports are often provided through the 15-pin MIDI/game port connector on most motherboards, on some multi-I/O boards, or on stand-alone game port adapter boards. When installing or enabling a game port, make sure that it is the *only* game port in the system. Multiple game ports will not crash the system because they do not use interrupts or DMA channels, but they will cause conflicts that prevent the joystick from responding properly. Attaching a joystick to a game port is as simple as plugging the joystick in and securing it with the two screws on the joystick cable.

Joystick software. Under DOS, joysticks are supported directly by each individual program—every game incorporates the code needed to access the game port and calibrate the joystick. Under Windows 95, you'll need to install drivers to support the joystick. If a joystick icon appears in your *Control Panel,* skip to the *Game Controller Setup* below. If you have not yet added your PC game port as New Hardware in the Windows 95 *Control Panel,* you should do this first:

1. Click the *Start* button.

2. Select *Settings,* then *Control Panel.*

3. In the *Control Panel,* look for a *Joystick* icon. If it's there, skip to the *Game Controller Setup.* If not, double-click the *Add New Hardware* icon to start the *Add New Hardware* wizard.

4. When prompted to have Windows search for new hardware, select *NO.* Click *Next* to continue.

5. Select *Sound, Video,* and *Game Controllers* and then click *Next.*

6. Select *Microsoft* as the Manufacturer and *Gameport Joystick* as the Model. This will add the game port as a device. Click *Next.*

7. If resource settings are given as 0201-0201, click *Next.* Windows will look for the required files. If it can't find these files, it will ask you to insert your Windows 95 CD or disk.

8. When the files have been installed, click *Finished.*

9. Shut down your computer and restart Windows 95.

Once your game port driver has been added, a joystick icon appears in your *Control Panel.* Use this to set up and calibrate your joystick, as follows:

1. Double-click on the *Joystick* icon in the *Control Panel*.

2. In the *Joystick Configuration* section, choose the appropriate joystick type from the list.

3. After selecting your *Joystick* configuration, click the *Calibration* button and carefully follow the on-screen instructions.

Joystick troubleshooting.   In spite of their simplicity, there are a number of problems that can be encountered with joysticks and game ports. The following symptoms outline some of the most common joystick issues.

Symptom 1: The joystick does not respond.   In most cases, the joystick is not installed properly. Make sure the joystick cable is not cut or damaged anywhere, and see that it is attached securely to the game port. It is the application that interrogates the joystick port. Examine the options or setup sections of your application and see that the control method is set to joystick rather than mouse or keyboard. Virtually all recent sound boards provide a 15-pin MIDI/joystick port in addition to the sound connections. If you are using the sound board port, make sure that the port is jumpered for use with a joystick (not MIDI). If you prefer to use a stand-alone joystick controller instead of the sound board's controller, see that the sound board's port is jumpered as a MIDI port—or disable the port outright. Also be sure that the game port's I/O address is set properly (i.e., 201h).

Symptom 2: The basic *X/Y,* two-button features of the joystick work, but the hat switch, throttle controls and supplemental buttons do not seem to respond.   In virtually all cases, the joystick is not configured properly. Many new applications provide several different joystick options and even allow you to define the particular use of each feature from within the application itself. Your joystick probably requires a supplemental definition file (i.e., an FCS file) in order to use all of the joystick's particular features. You may need a dual-port game port adapter. Some enhanced joysticks use both joystick positions (i.e., the X/Y axis and fire buttons make up one joystick, and the throttle and other buttons take up the other position). You may need to install a dual-port game port card.

Symptom 3: Joystick performance is erratic or choppy. This is usually a mechanical issue with the joystick itself. Make sure the joystick cable is not cut or damaged anywhere, and see that it is attached securely to the game port. Test a known-good joystick on the system. If a new joystick works as expected, the original joystick is worn out or damaged internally. Try recalibrating the joystick through the particular application. Make sure that there are no other devices in the system using the I/O address assigned to your game port (i.e., 201h). It is possible that the game port may be too slow for your particular system. This frequently occurs when older game port boards are used in very fast computers. Try a "speed adjusting" game port if you can.

Symptom 4: The joystick is sending incorrect information to the system—the joystick appears to be drifting. Either the application is not calibrating the joystick properly, or the game port is not adequate. Try recalibrating the joystick using your particular application. If the problem persists, try calibrating the joystick through a different application. If calibration works through one application, but problems persist in another, you may have a buggy application that needs a patch to update it. Make sure that there are no other devices in the system using the I/O address assigned to your game port (i.e., 201h). If drift issues continue with different applications, you may need to replace the game port adapter with a "low drift" or "speed adjusting" model.

Step 22: Installing a DVD-ROM drive

Today, the CD-ROM is showing its age, and a single CD no longer provides enough storage for the increasing demands of data-intensive applications. A new generation of high-density optical storage called DVD is now appearing. DVD technology promises to supply up to 17 Gbytes of removable storage on your desktop PC.

Specifications and standards. The next step in exploring DVD is to understand its various specifications, becoming familiar with the specifications that make DVD work and what a DVD will support. You don't need a lot of technical details, but you should recognize the most important points that you'll probably run across while reading documentation.

Access time. The *access time* is the time required for the drive to locate the required information on a disc. Optical drives like CD and DVD drives are relatively slow and can demand up to several hundred milliseconds to access information. For a DVD drive like the Creative Labs (Matsushita) DVD drive featured below, DVD access time is 470 ms (almost half a second), whereas access time for an ordinary CD is 180 ms. DVDs require so much more time because there is greater density of data. However, not all drives are as slow. The Toshiba DVD drive bundled with Diamond Multimedia's Maximum DVD Kit quotes a DVD access time of only 200 ms (130 ms for CDs).

Data transfer. Once data has been accessed, it must be transferred from the disc to the system. The *data transfer rate* measures how fast data can be read from the disc. There are two typical means of measuring the data rate: the speed at which data is read into the drive's on-board buffer (the *sequential* data transfer rate) and the speed at which data is transferred across the interface to the drive controller (the *buffered* data transfer rate). The Creative Labs (Matsushita) DVD drive offers a *sequential* data transfer rate of 1.35 Mbytes/s, and 900 kbytes/s for an ordinary CD (about equal to a 6X CD-ROM drive). By comparison the drive can support *buffered* data transfer rates of 8.3 Mbytes/s (DMA Mode 2), 13.3 Mbytes/s (DMA Mode 1), or 11.1 Mbytes/s (PIO Mode 3). As a result, the DVD-ROM drive is compatible with most EIDE drive controllers in the marketplace today.

Books and standards.   CD technology is defined by a set of accepted standards—we have come to know these as *books*. Because each CD book was bound with a different color jacket, each standard is referred to by color. For example, the standard that defines CD audio is called Red Book. Similarly, DVD technology is defined by a set of books. There are five books (labeled A through E) that relate to different applications:

- *Book A* defines the format and approach used for DVD-ROM (programs and data).

- *Book B* defines DVD-Video.

- *Book C* defines DVD-Audio (this specification is still under development).

- *Book D* defines DVD-WO (write once).

- *Book E* defines DVD-E (erasable or rewriteable) and DVD-RAM.

CD compatibility.   One of the most important aspects of any technology is backward compatibility—how well the new device will support your existing media. The same issue is true for DVD drives. Because DVD technology was designed as an improvement over existing CD-ROMs, the DVD *replaces* the CD-ROM rather than coexisting with it. Ideally, you'd remove your CD-ROM and replace it with a DVD-ROM drive. This means the DVD must be compatible with as many existing CD-ROM standards as possible. A typical DVD-ROM drive will support CD audio, CD-ROM, CD-I, CD Extra, CD-ROM/XA, and Video CD formats. Multisession formats such as Photo CD are not yet supported on all DVD drives.

> **NOTE:** One format that is *not* supported by any DVD drive yet is the Recordable CD (CD-R) format. The laser used in a DVD cannot read the CD-R and in some cases may even damage the CD-R disc. However, new CD-R blanks are being developed that should overcome this problem.

Caring for a DVD disc. As with CDs, a DVD disc is a remarkably reliable long-term storage media. Conservative expectations place the life estimates of a DVD disc at about 100 years. However, the longevity of an optical disc is affected by its storage and handling—a faulty CD can cause file and data errors that you might otherwise interpret as a defect in the drive itself. You can get the most life out of your optical disc by obeying the following rules:

- *Don't bend the disc.* Polycarbonate is a forgiving material, but you risk cracking or snapping (and thus ruining) the disc.

- *Don't heat the disc.* Remember, the disc is plastic. Leaving it by a heater or on the dashboard of your car will cause melting.

- *Don't scratch the disc.* Laser wavelengths have a tendency to "look past" minor scratches, but a major scratch can cause problems. Be especially careful of circular scratches (ones that follow the spiral track). A circular scratch can easily wipe out entire segments of data, which would be unrecoverable.

- *Don't use chemicals on the disc.* Especially don't use chemicals containing solvents such as ammonia, benzene, acetone, carbon tetrachloride, or chlorinated cleaning solvents. Such chemicals damage the plastic surface.

Eventually, a buildup of excessive dust or finger-prints can interfere with the laser beam enough to cause disc errors. When this happens, the disc can be cleaned easily using a dry, soft, lint-free cloth. Hold the disc by its edges and wipe radially (from hub to edge). *Do not wipe in a circular motion.* For stubborn stains, moisten the cloth in a bit of fresh isopropyl alcohol (*do not use water*). Place the cleaned disc in a caddie or jewel case for transport and storage.

Installing a DVD drive system. Typical DVD-ROM kits come complete with an EIDE or SCSI DVD-ROM drive, an MPEG-2 decoder board, a video loop-back cable, a CD audio cable, a line-input audio cable, and an IDE/EIDE or SCSI (40-pin) data cable. The actual installation process takes under an hour, but your installation may take longer depending on how much hardware you rearrange.

> **NOTE:** Before you attempt any new drive installation on your PC, be sure to perform a complete system back-up of your entire system and keep a bootable floppy disk handy in case of emergencies.

System considerations. Before you start any DVD installation, you'll need to meet some basic require-ments. DVD installation requires a 90-MHz Pentium PC with at least 16 Mbytes of RAM running Windows 95. At least 4 Mbytes of hard drive space will be need-ed for DVD drivers and application software, and your system's motherboard must have at least one PCI bus slot available for the MPEG-2 decoder board. Finally, there should be one open external drive bay available for the DVD-ROM drive itself.

There are two other issues that you need to consider before starting the installation. Consider your existing CD-ROM drive (there's almost certainly one in your system). Ideally, you'd like to remove the CD-ROM and install the DVD-ROM in its place. However, you may want to keep the CD-ROM in place if (1) you use CDs (such as Photo CDs) that you *know* the DVD-ROM drive will not support or (2) if you want to continue using DOS-based CDs. The DVD software and drivers do not support DOS, so you would lose all CD capability under DOS by removing the CD-ROM (that's one point that the DVD documentation leaves out).

Consider your DVD drive's interface. SCSI drives are rather straightforward; you can simply set the drive ID and then connect the drive directly to the SCSI cable (you may need to reterminate the SCSI cable). EIDE drives are a bit trickier. Most PCs today offer two IDE ports: a primary EIDE port that can support two EIDE devices and a secondary IDE port that can also support two devices. If you can, install the EIDE DVD-ROM as the slave device on the EIDE port (along side your hard drive). However, if you have two EIDE hard drives in the system, you should make the DVD drive the master device on the secondary IDE port. You may recall that older CD-ROM drives could present problems when used with hard drives, but DVD-drives use more current interfaces and should not interfere with an existing hard drive's operation.

Hardware installation. The hardware process basically consists of four steps: install the drive, cable the drive, install the decoder board, and cable the decoder board. Once the hardware is in place, you can then install the drivers and application software. If you've ever installed multimedia kits of CD-ROM drives and sound cards, installing a DVD-ROM kit should be a snap.

> **NOTE:** When working inside your PC, remember to keep the system turned off and unplugged. You should use a properly grounded antistatic wrist strap to remove any electrostatic charges from your body, but you should at least touch the PC's metal chassis regularly during the installation process just in case.

Install the drive.   Mount the DVD-ROM drive in an open drive bay, and secure it into place with four screws. As with all drives, be sure not to overtighten the screws. This could warp the drive just slightly and throw it out of alignment. Also check the jumpers on the rear of the drive. If the drive is SCSI, set the jumpers for the proper SCSI ID. For EIDE drives, set the drive as either master or slave. If you plan to run the drive along side a hard drive, set the DVD drive as slave. If you plan to run the DVD drive on its own controller port, set the DVD drive as master.

Cable the drive.   There are typically three cables that need to be connected to the DVD-ROM drive: a drive power cable, a data cable, and a CD audio cable. You can use any four-pin drive power cable but do not use a power cable from a Y-splitter. Splitting your power this way can sometimes cause erratic drive behavior. For slave drive configurations, you can connect the existing 40-pin signal cable to the data connector on the back of the drive (one end of the cable connects to the drive controller, one end connects to the hard drive, and the third unused connector attaches to the DVD drive. For master drive configurations, you can use the 40-pin cable that came with the DVD package. Finally, connect the CD audio cable between the DVD drive and the CD audio connector on your sound board. If you plan on leaving your existing CD-ROM in place, and playing any CD audio from the CD-ROM drive, don't connect the DVD drive's CD audio connector.

> **NOTE:** Remember to align pin 1 on the signal cable with pin 1 on the DVD drive. Pin 1 on a ribbon cable has a red or blue stripe that runs along the cable.

Install the decoder board.   Once the drive is in place, your next step is to install the MPEG-2 decoder board. You do not need to configure the decoder board first. The decoder is configured through software rather than with jumpers. Find an unused PCI bus slot, and mount the board—you may need to remove one of those little metal plates from the expansion slot opening first. You can use the little screw from that metal plate to secure the decoder board into place. Make sure that the board sits evenly and completely in its bus slot and *never* force an expansion board.

Cable the decoder board.   The last step is to inter-connect the MPEG-2 decoder board with the other devices in your system. In general, there are three con-nections that you have to make. Disconnect the moni-tor from your video board, and attach it to the decoder's Monitor connector. Use the loop-back cable to attach the video signal from your video board to the decoder's Video Input connector. Then use the sound cable to con-nect the decoder's Audio Output to the Line Input jack of your sound board.

Software installation.   One thing to note about the MPEG-2 decoder board is its lack of jumpers. The decoder packaged with a Creative Labs PC-DVD kit is configured exclusively through software. This simpli-fies the hardware installation process and reduces the chances of hardware conflicts due to incorrectly set jumpers. The software installation process involves three phases: installing the decoder drivers, installing the DVD-ROM drivers, and installing the DVD appli-cations.

The first time you reboot your PC after the hard-ware installation, Windows 95 will automatically detect the new hardware. It won't identify the hard-ware exactly, but it will identify the hardware as a PCI Multimedia Device. Insert the driver disk into your floppy drive, and elect to install the driver from "the disk provided by the manufacturer." Windows 95 will install the decoder board drivers and configure the board. When Windows 95 asks you to restart the system, choose *NO*.

The next step is to install the DVD-ROM drivers. Choose *Start,* and *Run,* and then type A:/SETUP. Click *OK.* The Setup routine will install the drivers for your DVD drive and configure it appropriately. When the installation is complete, Windows 95 will ask you again to restart the computer. This time, remove the driver disk and select *OK* to restart the computer. The next time Windows 95 starts, your DVD drive and decoder board should be active.

The last step is to install any DVD applications (such as a DVD control panel or DVD-Video player). The applications will usually be on a separate floppy disk. Insert the floppy disk, Click *Start,* and *Run,* and then type A:/SETUP. Then all you need to do is follow the instructions.

Basic DVD/MPEG-2 troubleshooting.   Even though a DVD package should install with an absolute minimum of muss and fuss, there are times when things just don't go according to plan. Software and hardware problems can interrupt your DVD system. The following symptoms cover some of the most common troubleshooting issues.

Symptom 1: The DVD drivers refuse to install.   This is almost always because Windows 95 is having a problem with one or more .INF files on your driver installation disk(s). Check with your DVD vendor to find out if you need to delete one or more entries in your OEMxx.INF file(s) (where xx is any suffix). You may also need to delete one or more entries from a MKED-VD.INF file. The .INF files are typically contained in the C:\WINDOWS\INF\OTHER directory. Once you've corrected the appropriate .INF file(s), you can reinstall the DVD drivers:

■ Click *Start,* select *Settings,* then click on *Control Panel.* Double-click on the *System* icon.

■ Click on the *Device Manager* tab, then select *Sound, Video, and Game Controllers.*

■ Select the DVD driver(s) and then click *Remove.*

- Exit the *Device Manager* and reinstall the drivers again.

Symptom 2: The DVD drive isn't detected. There are several possible reasons why the DVD drive would not be detected. Check the power connector attached to the drive, and make sure that the drive isn't being powered from a Y splitter power cable. Check the signal cable next. Both SCSI and EIDE signal cables must be attached securely to the drive. SCSI interfaces are complicated a bit by termination. Make sure that the drive is jumpered properly for its SCSI ID or EIDE master or slave relationship. Finally, make sure that the DVD drivers are installed and running. Check the drivers under the *Sound, Video, and Game Controllers* entry of your *Device Manager.*

Symptom 3: The DVD motorized tray won't open or close. The most common issue here is the DVD application itself. Some DVD applications (such as DVD-Video player applications) will "lock" the disc tray closed. Try closing all open applications. If the tray still won't open, try restarting the PC. This should clear any software lock. If the tray still refuses to open or close, the drive itself may be defective—you can force the tray open using a straightened paper clip in the emergency eject hole in the front of the drive.

Symptom 4: There is no audio when playing an audio CD. This is a common problem, especially during new DVD drive installations. Chances are that you did not connect the CD audio cable between the DVD drive and the sound board. If you did, the cable may be reversed (or defective). Of course, if you're still using your original CD-ROM drive, and the CD-ROM is connected to the sound board, there will be no CD audio from the DVD drive—there is no way to "parallel" the sound cable.

Symptom 5: There is no DVD audio while playing a movie or other presentation. Here's another common oversight during new DVD installations. Check the external audio cable attached between the MPEG-2 decoder board and the Line Input jack of your sound board. The cable may be plugged into the wrong jack(s), or the cable may be defective. Also check the sound board's mixer applet to see that the Line Input volume control setting is turned up to an acceptable level.

Symptom 6: Video quality appears poor. MPEG-2 compression is well-respected for its ability to reproduce high-quality images. The problem with poor image quality is almost always because of your video configuration—your color depth or resolution is too low. DVD-Video playback is best at resolutions of 800×600 or higher and at color depths of 16-bits (High Color) or higher (i.e., 24-bit True Color). In most cases, 256 colors will result in a dithered appearance.

Symptom 7: You see an error message that says "Disk playback unauthorized." The region code on the DVD disc does not match the code embedded into the drive. There isn't much that can be done when this error occurs. Note that region code limitations are only applied to DVD-Video movie releases—programs and data discs are not marked with region codes.

Step 23: Upgrading the BIOS

BIOS is referred to as *firmware*—software that is permanently encoded onto ICs. It provides the vital interface between the unique hardware designs of various motherboards and peripheral devices with standard operating systems such as Windows 95. Ideally, BIOS is designed to last for the life of the motherboard and should not need to be upgraded. However, BIOS is *still* essentially a piece of software and is subject to the same kinds of bugs and incompatibilities that operating systems and applications encounter. BIOS is normally upgraded under the following circumstances:

- An error or software bug has been detected in the BIOS that can cause the system to crash or important functions to fail (for example, improper disabling of an on-board video adapter is frequently the result of a BIOS error).

- The BIOS operates properly but cannot support new features, functions, or components that are appearing for an existing system (for example, supporting EIDE drives on an IDE system or supporting non-Intel CPUs often demands a BIOS update).

Updating a BIOS. There are two means of upgrading a BIOS: IC replacement and *flashing*. Traditionally, BIOS upgrades demand the replacement of the BIOS IC(s) on the motherboard. This means you'll need to order new BIOS ICs, remove the existing BIOS ICs, and then install the new ICs. Obviously, IC replacement is an invasive procedure that is best left to experienced PC enthusiasts and technicians. However, virtually all current motherboards use reprogrammable (flash) BIOS ICs instead of hard-coded ICs, so you can actually change the contents of flash BIOS on the fly without replacing any parts at all. Still, BIOS is absolutely critical to the operation of your motherboard, so no BIOS upgrade should be undertaken lightly.

> **NOTE:** Your PC will not function at all without a working BIOS. Problems with an upgrade (whether replacing or flashing an IC) can permanently disable your system. Make sure you have access to technical support and replacement BIOS ICs in the event of a BIOS upgrade failure.

A flash procedure. The following steps outline a typical flash BIOS procedure. The specific jumpers and command lines will probably be different, but the general procedure should be almost identical for all PCs:

1. After downloading the appropriate BIOS file from a BBS or Web site, extract it to a bootable MS-DOS 6.2x or Windows 95 disk.

2. Enter the CMOS Setup routine and record all of your CMOS settings to paper (take a <Print-Screen> of all your CMOS Setup pages). Also perform a complete system backup to tape or other removable media.

3. Turn the system off, open the cover, and set the flash BIOS protect jumper to the flash mode. Boot the system. If you are using MS-DOS 6.X, reboot your system with the bootable disk in the A: drive. To make sure a clean DOS environment is loaded, press the <F5> key when you see "Starting MS-DOS." After the system has rebooted, the A:\> prompt will appear. If you are using Windows 95, press <F8> when you see "Starting MS Windows 95." Select the *Safe Mode Command Prompt* option. Now you can run the FLASH utility from the A:\> prompt. For example, to update the Micronics Twister motherboard to BIOS version XX, you would type:

```
A:\>AWDFLASH TwisATX.BIN  <Enter>
```

4. After the FLASH screen appears, select *Yes* to save the current BIOS or *No* if you do not want to save the current BIOS (it is highly recommended that you save the current BIOS).

5. When prompted, select *Yes* to reprogram the BIOS.

6. After the update process has completed, you will be prompted to power off or reset your system. While power is off, reset the flash BIOS protect jumper to the protect mode. Close and secure the outer cover.

7. Reboot the system. Once the system reboots, verify that the new BIOS version appears on the screen. After reprogramming the BIOS, you will probably

need to enter Setup and restore your CMOS settings from your <PrintScreen> records.

NOTE: Some Windows 95 PnP systems use a portion of
CMOS RAM space to hold PnP data. When the CMOS
RAM is cleared during a BIOS upgrade, it may take the
PnP data with it. In some cases, you may be forced to
reinstall Windows 95 in order to restore the PnP config-
uration data.

Flash disasters. Although flashing a BIOS is typically
a fast, easy, and reliable process, there are times
when the procedure fails. Errors in the flash procedure can usually be caused by flashing the wrong
BIOS version for your PC, attempting to upgrade an
intermittent system, or losing system power during
the flash process. In any case, interruptions in the
flash procedure can leave your BIOS incompletely
updated. This is a *fatal* error for your system because
it will not boot if the BIOS checksum is wrong.

Recovering from a flash disaster. BIOS upgrade faults
are particularly serious because they will certainly
prevent your system from booting. There are three
solutions to this problem. First, you can replace the
actual physical BIOS IC(s) with properly programmed
ones. You'll need to buy the new ICs from the BIOS
maker, and it can take several days to obtain the new
ICs, which means your PC will be out of commission
for at least several days. Second, you can return the
entire motherboard to the system manufacturer and
let them restore the BIOS. This incurs a charge, but it
may be covered under the system's or motherboard's
warranty. A third solution is to use the BIOS Recovery
jumper on the motherboard to restore the original
BIOS code to the flash BIOS IC. This is a fairly new
feature that is appearing on motherboards such as the
Intel PC440FX motherboard, and it can dramatically
reduce technical support needed because of BIOS
upgrade faults.

Understanding CMOS Features

Some of the most frequent questions received at Dynamic Learning Systems involve the BIOS and the subtle meanings of the sometimes cryptic features supported by the BIOS. When you start your CMOS Setup routine to configure your PC, you'll find many odd entries whose meanings are not explained *any where*. Although the exact terms and feature set will vary between BIOS versions (and between BIOS makers), this appendix offers some explanations for basic and advanced CMOS entries that can help you configure your new PC properly and optimize it for top performance.

Main BIOS Setup Screen

The most important issue for a CMOS setup is the proper identification of drives and boot options that enable the system to start properly. This section describes the Setup options found on the Main menu. Keep in mind that certain options from the Main menu (such as Floppy Options) will cause Setup to switch to a submenu for specific settings under the selected option.

SYSTEM DATE: Specifies the current system date (month, day, and year). Usually entered manually or from a series of pop-up menus.

SYSTEM TIME: Specifies the current system time (hours and seconds). Usually entered manually.

FLOPPY OPTIONS: When selected, this displays the Floppy Options menu, which allows you to specify the types of floppy drives installed in the system (such as 5.25 or 3.5 in, double-density or high-density).

PRIMARY IDE MASTER: This reports if an IDE/EIDE device is connected to the Primary IDE/EIDE interface as the master. When selected, this displays the Primary IDE Master submenu.

PRIMARY IDE SLAVE: This reports if an IDE/EIDE device is connected to the Primary IDE/EIDE interface as the slave. When selected, this displays the Primary IDE Slave submenu.

SECONDARY IDE MASTER: This reports if an IDE/EIDE device is connected to the Secondary IDE/EIDE interface as the master. When selected, this displays the Secondary IDE Master submenu.

SECONDARY IDE SLAVE: This reports if an IDE/IDE device is connected to the Secondary IDE/EIDE interface as the slave. When selected, this displays the Secondary IDE Slave submenu.

LANGUAGE: Specifies the language of the text strings used in the Setup utility and the BIOS. The options are any installed languages. The number of available languages can vary greatly depending on the particular BIOS version.

BOOT OPTIONS: When selected, this displays the Boot Options submenu.

VIDEO MODE: This entry only reports the current video mode. There are no options to select.

MOUSE: This entry only reports if a mouse is installed or not. There are no options to select.

BASE MEMORY: This entry only reports the amount of base memory found. There are no options to select.

EXTENDED MEMORY: This entry only reports the amount of extended memory found. There are no options to select.

BIOS VERSION: This entry only reports the BIOS identification string (very handy when checking for potential BIOS upgrades). There are no options to select.

Floppy options menu

FLOPPY A: Shows if a "first" floppy disk drive is installed in the system. There are no options.

FLOPPY B: Shows if a "second" floppy disk drive is installed in the system. There are no options.

FLOPPY A: TYPE: Specifies the physical size and capacity of the "first" floppy disk drive. Typical options are:

- Disabled
- 360 kbytes, 5.25 in
- 1.2 Mbytes, 5.25 in
- 720 kbytes, 3.5 in
- 1.44/1.25 Mbytes, 3.5 in (default)
- 2.88 Mbytes, 3.5 in

FLOPPY B: TYPE: Specifies the physical size and capacity of the "second" floppy disk drive. The options are the same as those listed in the *Floppy A: Type* section above.

FLOPPY ACCESS: The BIOS displays this entry *only* if the motherboard supports changing the read/write or read-only access for floppy drives. When available, the following options change the access for *all* attached floppy drives:

- *Read / Write* (default)
- *Read Only*

Primary and secondary IDE menus

IDE DEVICE CONFIGURATION: Used to manually configure the hard drive (if the drive geometry is known) or
have the system autoconfigure it. The options are

- *Auto-Configured* (default)
- *User Definable*
- *Disabled*

If *User Definable* is selected, the *Cylinders, Heads,* and
Sectors options can be modified. If *Disabled* is selected,
the BIOS will not scan for a device on that interface.

CYLINDERS: If *IDE Device Configuration* is set to *Auto-
Configured,* this entry reports the number of cylinders
detected for your hard disk and cannot be modified. If
IDE Device Configuration is set to *User Definable,* you
must type the correct number of cylinders for your hard
disk.

HEADS: If *IDE Device Configuration* is set to *Auto-
Configured,* this entry reports the number of heads
detected for your hard disk and cannot be modified. If
IDE Device Configuration is set to *User Definable,* you
must type the correct number of heads for your hard
disk.

SECTORS: If *IDE Device Configuration* is set to *Auto-
Configured,* this entry reports the number of sectors
detected for your hard disk and cannot be modified. If
IDE Device Configuration is set to *User Definable,* you
must type the correct number of sectors for your hard
disk.

MAXIMUM CAPACITY: This entry only reports the maximum capacity of your hard disk, which is calculated
from the number of cylinders, heads, and sectors. There
are no options to select.

IDE TRANSLATION MODE: This specifies the IDE translation mode used with the IDE/EIDE hard drive. Typical
options are

- *Standard CHS* (standard cylinder, head, and sector addressing for IDE drives with fewer than 1024 cylinders).

- *Logical Block* (logical block addressing, or LBA, is not an option when *IDE Device Configuration* is set to *User Definable*).

- *Extended CHS* (extended cylinder, head, and sector addressing for drives with more than 1024 cylinders).

- *Auto-Detected* (BIOS detects type of translation mode—not an option when *IDE Device Configuration* is set to *User Definable*). (default)

   NOTE: Do not change the IDE translation mode from the option selected once the hard drive is formatted—changing the option *after* formatting can result in corrupted data.

   MULTIPLE SECTOR SETTING: Sets the number of sectors transferred by an IDE drive per interrupt request generated by the interface. Typical options are

- *Disabled*
- *Four sectors / block*
- *Eight sectors / block*
- *Autodetected* (default)

   NOTE: Check the specifications for your hard disk drive to determine which setting provides optimum performance for your drive.

   FAST PROGRAMMED I/O MODES: Sets how fast the data transfers occur across the IDE/EIDE interface. The options are

- *Disabled* (Data transfers occur at a less than optimized speed).

- *Auto-Detected* (Data transfers occur at the drive's maximum speed). (default)

Boot options menu

FIRST BOOT DEVICE: This option selects which drive the system checks *first* to find an operating system to boot from. Typical options are

- *Disabled*
- *Floppy* (default)
- *Hard Disk*
- *CD-ROM*
- *Network*

SECOND BOOT DEVICE: This option selects which drive the system checks *second* to find an operating system to boot from. Typical options are a bit more limited:

- *Disabled*
- *Floppy*
- *Hard Disk* (default)
- *Network*

THIRD BOOT DEVICE: This option (when available) selects which drive the system checks *third* to find an operating system to boot from. The options are the same as those listed for the Second Boot Device, but the default device is *Disabled*.

FOURTH BOOT DEVICE: This option (when available) selects which drive the system checks *fourth* to find an operating system to boot from. The options are the same as those listed for the Second Boot Device, but the default device is *Disabled*.

SYSTEM CACHE: This setting enables or disables both primary (L1) and secondary (L2) cache memory. The options are

- *Enabled* (default)
- *Disabled*

BOOT SPEED: This option selects the system speed at boot time. The options are

- *Deturbo* (motherboard operates at a slower speed to enable use of some legacy add-in cards).

- *Turbo* (motherboard operates at full speed). (default)

NUM LOCK: Sets the beginning state of the Num Lock feature on the numeric keypad of your keyboard at boot time. The options are

- *Off* (default)
- *On*

SETUP PROMPT: Controls whether the *Press <F1> Key if you want to run Setup* prompt is displayed during the power-up sequence. The options are

- *Disabled*
- *Enabled* (default)

NOTE: The *Setup Prompt* option does not affect your ability to access the Setup program. It only enables or disables the prompt.

HARD DISK PREDELAY: This option causes the BIOS to wait the specified period of time before it accesses the first hard drive. This is used when the drive type of a hard drive is not displayed during bootup, but the drive type is displayed following a warm boot (<Ctrl>+<Alt>+<Del>). The hard drive may need more time before it is able to communicate with the controller. Setting a predelay provides additional time for the hard drive to initialize. Typical options are

- *Disabled* (default)
- *3 s*
- *6 s*
- *9 s*

- *12 s*
- *15 s*
- *21 s*
- *30 s*

 Typematic Rate Programming: This option enables or disables the use of typematic rates. The options are

- *Default* (default)
- *Override* (lets you enter Typematic Rate Delay and Typematic Rate options)

 Typematic Rate Delay: Sets the delay time *before* the key-repeat function starts when you hold down a key on the keyboard. If the *Typematic Rate Programming* option is set to *Default,* this option is not visible. Typical options are

- *250 ms* (default)
- *500 ms*
- *750 ms*
- *1000 ms*

 Typematic Rate: This is the speed at which characters repeat when you hold down a key on the keyboard. The higher the number, the faster the characters repeat. If the *Typematic Rate Programming* option is set to the *Default,* this option is not visible. Typical options are

- *6 characters per second* (default)
- *8 characters per second*
- *10 characters per second*
- *12 characters per second*
- *15 characters per second*
- *20 characters per second*
- *24 characters per second*

■ *30 characters per second*

> SCAN USER FLASH AREA: This option scans the user flash area for an executable binary to be executed during POST and is used to enable the BIOS flash process. The options are

■ *Disabled* (no scan). (default)

■ *Enabled* (scan occurs during POST).

> **NOTE:** Regardless of the setting of this option, if an OEM logo is programmed into the user flash area, the logo will be displayed at bootup.

> POWER-ON COM1 RING: This option enables the system to power on when a telephony device configured for operation on COM1 receives an incoming Plain Old Telephone Service (POTS) call. The options are

■ *Disabled* (default)

■ *Enabled*

> **NOTE:** This item typically does not appear if an *Auto Start on AC Loss* option is disabled.

Advanced Setup Menu

The main Setup menus primarily deal with drives and booting issues, but there are many options that are specific to the chipset or motherboard design that are handled through an advanced menu scheme. The advanced menus usually handle peripheral configurations, chipset-specific options, power management, PnP options, and event-logging features (if included in the BIOS version).

> PROCESSOR TYPE: This entry only reports the processor type detected in the system. There are no options to select.

> PROCESSOR SPEED: This entry only reports the processor clock speed (or bus speed) set for the system. There are no options to select.

CACHE SIZE: This entry only reports the size of the secondary (L2 or external) cache detected in the system. There are no options to select.

PERIPHERAL CONFIGURATION: When selected, this option displays the *Peripheral Configuration* submenu.

ADVANCED CHIPSET CONFIGURATION: When selected, this option displays the *Advanced Chipset Configuration* submenu.

POWER MANAGEMENT CONFIGURATION: When selected (and power management is enabled), this option displays the *Advanced Power Management* submenu.

PLUG-AND-PLAY CONFIGURATION: When selected, this option displays the *Plug-and-Play Configuration* submenu.

EVENT LOGGING CONFIGURATION: When selected, this option displays the *Event Logging Configuration* submenu.

Peripheral configuration menu

PRIMARY PCI IDE INTERFACE: This option is used to automatically configure or disable the primary PCI IDE hard disk interface. The options are

- *Disabled*
- *Auto-Configured* (default)

SECONDARY PCI IDE INTERFACE: This option is used to automatically configure or disable the secondary PCI IDE hard disk interface. The options are

- *Disabled*
- *Auto-Configured* (default)

FLOPPY INTERFACE: This option disables or automatically configures the floppy disk drive interface. The options are

■ *Disabled*

■ *Enabled*

■ *Auto-Configured* (default)

> SERIAL PORT 1 INTERFACE: This feature selects the logical COM port, I/O address, and interrupt for Serial Port 1. The options that are displayed may vary depending on whether you choose Windows 95 as the PnP OS screen. The typical options are

■ *Disabled*

■ *<COMx>, <I/O address>, <IRQx>* (the port is configured manually).

■ *Auto-Configured* (Setup assigns the first free COM port: normally COM1, 3F8h, IRQ4.) (default)

> SERIAL PORT 2 INTERFACE: This feature selects the logical COM port, I/O address, and interrupt for serial port 2. The options that are displayed may vary depending on whether you choose Windows 95 as the PnP OS screen. The typical options are

■ *Disabled*

■ *<COMx>, <I/O address>, <IRQx>* (the port is configured manually).

■ *Auto-Configured* (setup assigns the first free COM port: normally COM2, 2F8h, IRQ3). (default)

> **NOTE:** If you specifically set either serial port address, that address will not appear in the list of options for the other serial port. If an ATI Mach32 or an ATI Mach64 video controller is active (as an add-in card), the COM4, 2E8h address will not appear in the list of options for either serial port.

> SERIAL PORT 2 IR INTERFACE: This option (if available on the motherboard) controls the IR port that makes serial port 2 available to infrared applications. The options are

- *Disabled* (default)
- *Enabled*

    PARALLEL PORT INTERFACE: This selects the logical print-
    er port, I/O address, interrupt, and DMA channel (if
    applicable) of the parallel port. The options that are
    displayed may vary depending on the parallel port type
    you choose (see below) and whether you choose
    Windows 95 as the PnP OS. Typical options appear in
    the following format:

- *Disabled*
- *<LPTx>, <I/O address>, <IRQx>, <DMAx>*
- *Auto-Configured* (Setup assigns LPT1, 378h, IRQ7).
  (default)

    NOTE: The <DMAx> will appear only if the *Parallel
    Port Type* item is set to *Extended Capability Port* (ECP).

    PARALLEL PORT TYPE: This option selects the mode for
    your parallel port. The choice of parallel port mode can
    affect printer performance, as well as that of other par-
    allel port devices. Typical options are

- *Compatible* (operates in AT-compatible mode)
  (default)
- *Bidirectional* (operates in bidirectional PS/2-com-
  patible mode)
- *EPP* (Enhanced Parallel Port, a high-speed bidirectional mode)
- *ECP* (Extended Capabilities Port, a high-speed
  bidirectional mode)

    USB INTERFACE: This option enables or disables the
    USB interface. USB support requires that the BIOS
    allocate a PCI interrupt, which could cause an inter-
    rupt to be shared with another device. If interrupt
    sharing is a problem (and you do not need support for a
    USB), you can free an interrupt by disabling USB out-
    right. Options are

- *Disabled* (frees the PCI interrupt used to support USB)
- *Enabled* (default)

  AUDIO INTERFACE: If there is an audio subsystem built into your motherboard, this option enables or disables the on-board audio subsystem. If there is no on-board sound system, this option will not appear. The options are

- *Disabled* (select before installing a sound board)
- *Enabled* (default)

  HARDWARE MONITOR INTERFACE: This option displays only if the hardware monitor component is recognized on the motherboard, and it enables or disables the hardware monitor feature. If available, The options are

- *Disabled*
- *Enabled* (default)

  PRIMARY PCI IDE STATUS: This entry only reports if the primary IDE interface is enabled or disabled. There are no other options to select.

  SECONDARY PCI IDE STATUS: This entry only reports if the secondary IDE interface is enabled or disabled. There are no other options to select.

  FLOPPY STATUS: This entry only reports if the floppy disk drive interface is enabled or disabled. There are no other options to select.

  SERIAL PORT 1 STATUS: This entry only reports the COM port, I/O address, and IRQ for serial port 1. There are no other options to select.

  SERIAL PORT 2 STATUS: This entry only reports the COM port, I/O address, and IRQ for serial port 2. There are no other options to select.

  PARALLEL PORT STATUS: This entry only reports the logical printer port, I/O address, and IRQ for the parallel port. There are no other options to select.

Advanced chipset menu

BASE MEMORY SIZE: This entry sets the size of the base (conventional) memory. The options are

- 512 kbytes
- 640 kbytes (default)

ISA LFB SIZE: This entry sets the size of the linear frame buffer used with some ISA adapter cards. The options are

- *Disabled* (default)
- *1 Mbytes*
- *2 Mbytes*
- *4 Mbytes*

ISA LFB BASE ADDRESS: If an *ISA LFB Size* is selected, the *ISA LFB Base Address* field appears. This entry reports the base address of the Linear Frame Buffer (LFB). There are no options. This entry does not appear if the *ISA LFB Size* is set to *Disabled.*

VIDEO PALETTE SNOOP: This option controls the ability of a primary PCI graphics controller to share a common palette with an ISA add-in video card. This option is typically disabled because it is extremely unusual for PCI and ISA video cards to coexist in a system. The options are

- *Disabled* (default)
- *Enabled*

ISA VGA WRITE COMBINING: This option determines whether VGA frame buffer addresses (B000h to BFFFh) are set to the processor's "write combined" memory type:

- *Disabled* (not set to write combined type) (default)
- *Enabled* (set to write combined type)

LATENCY TIMER (PCI CLOCKS): This option sets the length of time that a device on the PCI bus can hold the bus after another device requests it. The entries are multiples of 8 ranging from 16 up to 128 (i.e., 16, 24, and so on up to 128). The latency value is autoconfigured by default and is obtained by three possible methods:

- On-board device. The optimum latency value is known and that value is used.

- Minimum grant register of device is nonzero. Use that value to derive the latency value.

- Minimum grant register of device is 0. Use latency value of 20h.

MEMORY ERROR DETECTION: This option sets the type of memory-error detection or correction for main memory. This entry appears if either ECC or parity memory is detected. Parity and ECC memory may be configured to run either as parity or ECC (parity memory may be configured to run in ECC mode). This item does not appear if the memory detected by the BIOS does not support ECC or parity. The options are

- *Disabled* (default)
- *ECC*
- *Parity*

BANK 0: This entry only reports the type of memory found in the first bank. There are no other options to select.

BANK 1: This entry only reports the type of memory found in the second bank. There are no other options to select.

Power management menu

ADVANCED POWER MANAGEMENT: This option enables or disables Advanced Power Management (APM) support in the BIOS. APM manages power consumption only when used with an APM-capable operating system (such as Windows 95). The options are

- *Disabled* (only the option *Auto Start On AC Loss* appears)
- *Enabled* (default)

IDE DRIVE POWER DOWN: This option sets any IDE/EIDE drives to spin down when the computer goes into a power managed mode. The options are

- *Disabled*
- *Enabled* (default)

VESA VIDEO POWER DOWN: This option sets any VESA-compliant monitor to use its own internal power management when the system goes into a power managed mode. The typical options are

- *Disabled* (the monitor is not under power management).
- *Standby* (minimal power reduction, HSYNC signal not active).
- *Suspend* (significant power reduction, VSYNC signal not active).
- *Sleep* (maximum power reduction, HSYNC and VSYNC not active). (default)

INACTIVITY TIMER: This option selects the number of minutes the computer must be inactive before it enters its power managed mode. The range is 0 to 255 min. The default is 10 min.

HOT KEY: This entry sets up the hot key that controls the power managed mode. When a user presses this key while holding down the <Ctrl> and <Alt> keys, the system enters its power managed mode. All alphabetic keys are valid entries for this field. The BIOS must be using an operating system-dependent APM driver for this option to work.

NOTE: If you set the APM hot key and the security hot key to the same key, the APM function has priority.

AUTO START ON AC LOSS: This feature enables returning to the last known state of the system or powering down the system if the motherboard detects that AC power to the power supply is lost. The options are

- *Disabled*
- *Enabled* (default)

Plug-and-Play configuration menu

CONFIGURATION MODE: This option selects how the BIOS gets information about ISA cards that do not have PnP capabilities (legacy cards). The options are

- *Use BIOS Setup* (displays options for reserving resources for ISA legacy devices)

- *Use PnP OS* (displays a choice of operating systems as listed in the following section) (default)

PnP OS: This option applies only to ISA cards; the BIOS always autoconfigures PCI devices. The option lets the computer boot with an operating system capable of managing PnP add-in cards. If you choose either the option *Other* or *Windows 95,* the BIOS assigns resources to ISA PnP Initial Program Load (IPL) devices. The operating system is then responsible for enabling devices and assigning resources (i.e., I/O addresses and interrupts) for all remaining devices. The options are

- *Disabled* (for DOS; BIOS configures and enables all devices at boot time, whether or not they are PnP).

- *Other PnP OS* (BIOS autoconfigures PCI devices before on-board motherboard devices).

- *Windows 95* (BIOS autoconfigures on-board motherboard devices before PCI devices). (default)

ISA SHARED MEMORY SIZE: This option lets you specify a
range of memory addresses that ISA add-in cards can
use for shared memory, but these addresses will not be
used for shadowing ROM memory from other devices.
Enable this feature when using a legacy ISA add-in
card without PnP capabilities only and when the card
requires memory space that is not in ROM. For example, this could include Local Area Network (LAN) cards
that have on-board memory buffers or video capture
cards that have video-buffer memory. By default, upper
memory is allocated as follows: Memory from C0000 to
C7FFFh is automatically shadowed (this memory range
is typically reserved for video BIOS), and memory from
C8000h to DFFFFh is initially unshadowed.

The BIOS scans this range for any ISA add-in cards
that may be present and notes their location and size.
The BIOS then autoconfigures the PCI and PnP
devices, shadowing their ROM requirements (other
than video) into the area above E0000h. If that area
becomes full, it continues shadowing to the area
between C8000h and DFFFFh. If an ISA legacy card
has memory requirements that are not in ROM, the
autoconfigure routine might write into an area that is
needed by the ISA card. Use the *ISA Shared Memory
Size* and *ISA Shared Memory Base Address* entries to
reserve a block of memory that will not be used for
shadowing. Typical options are

- *Disabled* (The ISA Shared Memory Base Address
  field does not appear). (default)
- *16 kbytes*
- *32 kbytes*
- *48 kbytes*
- *64 kbytes*
- *80 kbytes*
- *96 kbytes*

ISA SHARED MEMORY BASE ADDRESS: This entry selects
the base address for the *ISA Shared Memory*. The

options that appear depend on the *ISA Shared Memory Size* entry. The total amount of ISA shared memory cannot extend to the E0000h address. For example, if you specify a size of 64 kbytes, options D4000h, D8000h, and DC000h will not be available. The typical options are

- *C8000h* (default)
- *CC000h*
- *D0000h*
- *D4000h*
- *D8000h*
- *DC000h*

  IRQ 3-15: This option sets the status of each IRQ for configuration purposes. The PCI autoconfiguration code uses these settings to determine whether these interrupts are available for use by PCI add-in cards. If an interrupt is marked "available," the autoconfiguration code can assign the interrupt to be used by the system. If your computer has an ISA add-in card that requires an interrupt, select *Used By ISA Card* for that interrupt. The options are

- *Available* (default)
- *Used by ISA Card*

  NOTE: IRQs 5, 9, 10, and 11 are the default user-available IRQs. Depending on the configuration of your computer, other IRQs may be listed (for example, if you disable the parallel port and/or serial ports).

Event logging menu

  EVENT LOG CAPACITY: This information entry lists whether the log is full or not. There are no options to select.

  EVENT COUNT GRANULARITY: This information entry tells the number of log events that will occur before the event log is updated. There are no options to select.

EVENT TIME GRANULARITY (MINUTES): This information entry tells the number of minutes that will pass before the event log is updated. There are no options to select.

EVENT LOG CONTROL: This feature enables event logging (when available). Typical options are

- *All Events Enabled* (default)
- *ECC Events Disabled*
- *All Events Disabled*

CLEAR EVENT LOG: This option sets a flag that clears the event log the next time the POST runs. The typical options are

- *Keep* (the event log will not be cleared). (default)
- *On Next Boot* (the event log will be cleared).

MARK EXISTING EVENTS AS READ: This option sets a flag that marks all events in the log as having been read the next time the POST runs. The typical options are

- *Do Not Mark* (events will not be marked as read). (default)
- *Mark* (all events will be marked as read).

EVENT LOG SUBSCREENS: The bottom of the *Event Log* screen includes several information fields. These fields display information about the last event of a specific type and a count of how many events of that type are logged. Selecting a field and pressing the <Enter> key displays a subscreen that shows information specific to that type of event. Table A.1 lists the event types that are available. The subscreens for all event types include the initial three lines of information (date, time, and total count) as shown for single-bit ECC events.

NOTE: These logs show the last recorded event, which may *not* be from this boot session unless you automatically clear the event log at bootup.

TABLE A.1 Common Event Log Subscreens

Event type	Subscreen detail
Single-bit ECC events	Date of Last Occurrence None (initial value)
Multiple-bit ECC events	Time of Last Occurrence None (initial value)
Parity error events	Total Count of Events/Errors None (initial value)
	Memory Bank with Errors None (initial value)
Preboot events	Date of Last Occurrence None (initial value)
	Time of Last Occurrence None (initial value)
	Total Count of Events/Errors None (initial value)

Security Menu

System security is a growing concern for all levels of computer user, and BIOS is becoming more sophisticated in its use of password protection. This section describes the BIOS options that can be set to restrict access to both the Setup program and the computer. An *administrative* password and a *user* password can be entered for the Setup program *and* for booting the computer. Table A.2 illustrates the effects of administrative and user passwords (this table is for reference only and is not displayed on the screen).

USER PASSWORD: This entry only reports if there is a user password set. There are no options to select.

ADMINISTRATIVE PASSWORD: This entry only reports if there is an administrative password set. There are no options to select.

ENTER PASSWORD: This option sets the user password, which can be up to seven alphanumeric characters in length.

TABLE A.2 Administrative and User Password Functions

Password set	Administrative mode	User mode	Setup options	Password to enter setup	Password during boot
Neither	Can change all options*	Can change all options*	None	None	None
Administrative only	Can change all options	Can change a limited number of options†	Administrative Password User Privilege Level	Administrative	None
User only	N/A	Can change all options	Enter Password Clear User Password	User	User
Administrative and user set	Can change all options	Can change a limited number of options†	Administrative Password User Privilege Level Enter Password	Administrative or user	Administrative or user

*If no password is set, any user can change all Setup options.
†The level of user access is set with the *User Privilege Level* option (see text below).

SET ADMINISTRATIVE PASSWORD: This option sets the administrative password, which can be up to seven alphanumeric characters in length.

USER PRIVILEGE LEVEL: This option sets the level of access users can have to the Setup program. This option can be set only by an administrative user with access to the administrative password. This option is only displayed when the administrative password is set. Table A.3 specifies Setup access for each option. The options are

- *Limited Access* (default)
- *No Access*
- *View Only*
- *Full Access*

CLEAR USER PASSWORD: This option clears the current user password. The user password must be set with Enter Password *first* in order to enable this entry.

UNATTENDED START: Controls when the security password is requested. The user password must be set first in order to enable this entry. The options are

- *Enabled* (the system boots, but the keyboard is locked until the user password is entered).
- *Disabled* (the system does not boot until the user password is entered). (default)

SECURITY HOT KEY: This option sets up a hot key that locks the keyboard until the user password is entered. All alphabetic keys are valid entries for this field. When a user presses this key while holding down the <Ctrl> and <Alt> keys, the keyboard locks and the keyboard LEDs flash to indicate that the keyboard is locked. When you enter the user password to unlock the keyboard, you do not have to press <Enter>.

NOTE: If you set the Security and APM hot keys (see under the "Power Management Menu" heading above) to the same key, the APM function has priority.

TABLE A.3 **Access for User Privilege Level Options**

Option	Access
Limited access	Users can access the Setup program and can change the following options: System Date, System Time, User Password, Unattended Start, and Security Hot-Key. Other Setup options are not visible.
No access	Users cannot access the Setup program.
View only	Users can access the Setup program and view options but cannot change any options.
Full access	Users can access the Setup program and can change all options except User Privilege Level and Set Administrative Password.

Exit Menu

Once you have made changes to your CMOS Setup, you must still exit the Setup routine and reboot the system so that your changes can take effect. However, there are a number of options available when exiting a CMOS Setup routine, so this part of the appendix explains the various exiting options that are available.

EXIT SAVING CHANGES: This option exits Setup and saves the changes in CMOS RAM. You can also press the <F10> key at any time in the Setup program to do this.

EXIT DISCARDING CHANGES: This option exits Setup without saving any changes. This means that any changes you have made while in Setup are discarded and not saved. Pressing the <Esc> key in any of the four main screens will also exit and discard changes.

LOAD SETUP DEFAULTS: This option returns all of the Setup options to their default values. The default Setup values are loaded from the ROM table. You can also press the <F5> key anywhere in Setup to load the defaults.

DISCARD CHANGES: This option discards any changes made up to this point in Setup without exiting the

Setup routine. This selection loads the CMOS RAM values that were present when the system was turned on. You can also press the <F6> key anywhere in Setup to discard changes.

B

Summary of Current Standards

As you select parts for your new PC, you're going to encounter an array of various standards and specifications used in modern PCs. This appendix highlights the most important standards.

Specification	Description	Revision level and sponsors
APM	*Advanced Power Management* BIOS interface specification (for motherboard power conservation)	Revision 1.2, February 1996, Intel Corporation, Microsoft Corporation (www.intel.com)
ATA-3	Information Technology *AT Attachment-3 Interface* (for enhanced drive performance)	X3T10/2008D Revision 6, ATA Anonymous FTP Site: (fission.dt.wdc.com)
ATAPI	*ATA Packet Interface* for CD-ROMs (allows non-HDD devices to use the IDE interface)	SFF-8020i Revision 2.5 (SFF) Fax Access: (408) 741-1600

Specification	Description	Revision level and sponsors
ATX	*ATX form factor speci-fication* (standard dimensioning for cases, motherboards, and power supplies)	Revision 2.01, February 1997 Intel (www.intel.com)
DMI	*Desktop Management Interface* BIOS speci-fication	Version 2.0, October 16, 1995 American Mega-trends Award Soft-ware, Dell Computer, Intel, Phoenix Tech-nologies, SystemSoft
"El Torito"	*Bootable CD-ROM* for-mat specification	Version 1.0, January 25, 1995 Phoenix Technologies, IBM. The "El Torito" specifi-cation is available on the Phoenix Web site; (www.ptltd.com/techs/specs.html)
EPP	*Enhanced Parallel Port*	IEEE 1284 standard, Mode [1 or 2], v1.7
IrDA	*Serial Infrared* Physical Layer Link specification	Version 1.1, October 17, 1995 Infrared Data Association
Management extension hardware	LM78 Microprocessor System Hardware Monitor	Current Web site: (www.national.com/pf/LM/LM78.html)
PCI	*PCI Local Bus* specifi-cation	Revision 2.1, June 1, 1995 PCI Special Interest Group
Plug and Play	*Plug and Play* BIOS specification	Version 1.0a, May 5, 1994 Compaq, Phoenix Technologies, Intel
USB	*Universal Serial Bus* specification	Revision 1.0, January 15, 1996 Compaq, Digital, IBM, Intel, Microsoft, NEC, Northern Telecom

PC Preventive Maintenance

For most users, the purchase or construction of a new PC is a substantial investment of both time and money. But after the money is spent and the PC is in our home or office, few of us ever take the time to *maintain* our PC. Routine maintenance is an important part of PC ownership and can go a long way toward keeping your computer's hardware *and* software error-free. Proper routine maintenance can also help to avoid costly visits to your local repair shop. This appendix provides you with a comprehensive step-by-step procedure for protecting and maintaining your personal computer investment.

Protecting Your Data

It's interesting to note that the data recorded on our computer is often far more valuable than the actual cost of a new drive. But if the drive fails, our precious data is usually lost along with the hardware. Months (perhaps years) of records and data could be irretrievably lost with the failure of just a few bytes on a hard drive. One of the first steps in any routine maintenance plan is to make regular *backups* of your system's contents—as well as the system's configuration. Backups ensure that you can recover from any hardware glitch, accidental file erasure, or virus attack.

Step 1: File backups

File backups are important for all types of PC user from major corporations to occasional home users. By creating a copy of your system files (or even just a part of them), you can restore the copy and continue working in the event of a disaster. Before you proceed with any type of system checks, consider performing a file backup.

What you need.   You're going to need two items in order to back up your files: a backup drive and backup software. The actual choice of backup drive is really quite open. Tape drives such as the Iomega Ditto drive (www.iomega.com) or the MicroSolutions 8000t 8GB Backpack drive (www.micro-solutions.com) are the traditional choice, but other high-volume removable media drives like Iomega's 100-Mbyte Zip drive, their 1-Gbyte Jaz drive, or the SyQuest 1.5GB EZ-Flyer drive (www.syquest.com) are very popular. You may choose an internal or external version of a drive, but you might consider an *external* parallel port drive because it is portable—it can be shared with other PCs.

You'll also need some backup software to format the media and handle your backup and restore operations. If you're using Windows 95, try the native Backup applet (click on *Start, Programs, Accessories, System Tools,* and *Backup*). If Backup doesn't suit your needs, many drives ship with a backup utility on disk. Just make sure that the backup drive and backup software are compatible with one another.

Types of backups. Backups generally fall into two categories: incremental and complete. Both types of backups offer unique advantages and disadvantages. An *incremental* backup only records the changes since the last backup. This usually results in a faster backup procedure and uses less tape (or other media), but restores take longer because you need to walk through each "increment" in order. A *complete* backup records the drive's full contents. This takes much longer and uses a lot more media, but restores are easier. Many PC users employ a combination of complete and incremental backups. For example, you might start with a complete backup on January 1 and then make incremental backups each week until the end of February. By March 1, you'd make another complete backup and start the incremental backup process again.

Backup frequency. Perhaps the most overlooked issue with backups is the frequency. How often should backups be performed? The answer to that question is not always a simple one because everyone's needs are different. Major corporations with busy order entry systems may back up several times each day, whereas individual home users may not even consider backups to be necessary. The standard that I use is this: Can you afford to lose the data on this drive? if the answer is No, it's time to back up.

File backup tips. Regardless of how you choose to handle file backups, there are some tips that will help you get the most from your backup efforts:

- Keep the backup(s) in a secure location (such as a fireproof safe or cabinet).

- Keep the backup(s) in a different physical location, away from the original PC.

- Back up consistently. Backups are useless if they are out of date.

- If time is a factor, start with a complete backup and then use incremental backups.

- Use a parallel port tape drive (or other backup drive) for maximum portability between PCs.

Step 2: CMOS backups

All PCs use a sophisticated set of configuration settings (everything from Date and Time to Video Palette Snoop and Memory Hole) that define how the system should be operated. These settings are stored in a small amount of very low-power memory called CMOS RAM (you can learn more about CMOS Setup variables in App. A). Each time the PC starts, motherboard BIOS reads the CMOS RAM and copies the contents into low system memory—also known as the BIOS Data Area, or BDA. While system power is off, CMOS RAM contents are maintained with a small battery. If this battery goes dead, CMOS contents can be lost. In most cases, this will prevent the system from even starting until you reconfigure the CMOS Setup from scratch. By making a backup of the CMOS Setup, you can restore lost settings in a matter of minutes. CMOS backups are simply printed screens of your CMOS Setup pages.

What you need.   The one item that you'll need to perform a CMOS backup is a *printer*. It really doesn't matter what kind of printer (i.e., dot-matrix, ink jet, or laser). The printer should be attached to the PC's parallel port. After starting the CMOS Setup routine, visit each page of the Setup and use the <Print Screen> key to capture each page to the printer. Because every BIOS is written differently, be sure to check for submenus that might be buried under each main menu option.

CMOS backup tips.   CMOS backups are quick and simple, but you'll get the most benefit from a CMOS backup by following the pointers below:

- Make it a point to print out *every* CMOS Setup page.

- Keep the printed pages taped to the PC's housing or with the system's original documentation.

- Back up the CMOS Setup whenever you make a change to the system's configuration.

Cleaning

Now that you've backed up the system's vital information, you can proceed with the actual maintenance procedures. The first set of procedures involve exterior cleaning. This may hardly sound like a glamorous process, but you'd be surprised how quickly dust, pet hair, and other debris can accumulate around a computer. You'll need four items for cleaning: a supply of Windex or other mild ammonia-based cleaner (a little ammonia in water will work just as well), a supply of paper towels or clean lint-free cloths, a canister of electronics-grade compressed air, which can be obtained from any electronics store, and a small static-safe vacuum cleaner.

> **NOTE:** Avoid the use of ordinary household vacuum cleaners. The rush of air tends to generate significant amounts of static electricity along plastic hoses and tubes, which can accidentally damage the sensitive electronics in a PC.
> **NOTE:** *Never* use harsh or industrial-grade cleaners around a PC. Harsh cleaners often contain chemicals that can damage the finish of (or even melt) the plastics used in PC housings. Use a highly diluted ammonia solution *only*.

As a rule, exterior cleaning can be performed every 4 months (three times per year) or as required. If the PC is operating in dusty, industrial, or other adverse environments, you many need to clean the system more frequently. Systems operating in clean office environments may only need to be cleaned once or twice each year. Always remember to turn off the com-

puter and unplug the AC cord from the wall outlet
before cleaning.

Step 3: Clean the case

Use a clean cloth lightly dampened with ammonia
cleaner to remove dust, dirt, or stains from the exteri-
or of the PC. Start at the top and work down. Add a
little bit of extra cleaner to remove stubborn stains.
You'll find that the housing base is typically the dirti-
est (especially for tower systems). When cleaning, be
careful not to accidentally alter the CD-ROM volume
or sound card master volume controls. Also do not dis-
lodge any cables or connectors behind the PC.

> **NOTE:** Always dampen a clean towel with cleaner.
> *Never* spray cleaner directly onto any part of the com-
> puter.

Step 4: Clean the air intake

While cleaning the case, pay particular attention to
the air intake(s), which are usually located in the
front (or front sides) of the housing. Check for accumulations of dust or debris around the intakes or
caught in an intake filter. Clean away any accumulations from the intake area and then use your static-
safe vacuum to clean the intake filter if possible. You
may need to remove the intake filter for better access.
If the intake filter is washable, you may choose to
rinse the filter in simple soap and water for best
cleaning (remember to dry the filter thoroughly before
replacing it). Of course, if there is no intake filter, simply clean around the intake area.

Step 5: Clean the speakers

Multimedia speakers offer a countless number of
ridges and openings that are just perfect for accumu-
lating dust and debris. Use your can of compressed air
to gently blow out the speaker's openings. Do not

insert the long, thin air nozzle into the speaker. You can easily puncture the speaker cone and ruin it. Instead, remove the long nozzle and spray air directly from the can. Afterward, use a clean cloth lightly dampened with ammonia solution to remove any dirt or stains from the speaker housings.

Step 6: Clean the keyboard

Keyboards are open to the environment, so dust and debris readily settle between the keys. Over time, these accumulations can jam keys, or cause repeated keystrokes. Attach the long thin nozzle to your can of compressed air, and use the air to blow through the horizontal gaps between key rows. Be careful—this will kick up a lot of dust, so keep the keyboard away from your face. Afterward, use a clean cloth lightly dampened with ammonia solution to remove dirt or stains from the keys and keyboard housing. If any keys seem unresponsive or stick, you can remove the corresponding keycap and spray a bit of good-quality electronic contact cleaner into the key assembly and then gently replace the keycap.

> **NOTE:** Do not remove the <Enter> key or <Space Bar>. These keys are held in place by metal brackets that are *extremely* difficult to reattach once the key is removed. Only the most experienced technicians should work with these keys.

Step 7: Clean the monitor

There are several important issues when cleaning a monitor: ventilation, case, and CRT. Monitors rely on vent openings for proper cooling. Use your vacuum cleaner and carefully remove any accumulations of dust and debris from the vents underneath the case, as well as those on top of the case. Make sure that none of the vent openings are blocked by paper or other objects (this can restrict ventilation and force the monitor to run hot).

Next, use a clean cloth lightly dampened with ammonia solution to clean the monitor's plastic case. There is active circuitry directly under the top vents, so under no circumstances should you spray cleaner directly onto the monitor housings. Do *not* use ammonia or *any* chemicals to clean the CRT face. The CRT is often treated with antiglare and other coatings, and even mild chemicals can react with some coatings. Instead, use clean tap water *only* to clean the CRT face. Be sure to dry the CRT face completely.

Step 8: Clean the mouse

Like the keyboard, a mouse is particularly susceptible to dust and debris, which are carried from the mouse pad up into the mouse ball and rollers. When enough foreign matter has accumulated, you'll find that the mouse cursor hesitates or refuses to move completely. Loosen the retaining ring and remove the mouse ball. Clean the mouse ball using a clean cloth and an ammonia solution. Dry the mouse ball thoroughly and set it aside with the retaining ring. Next, locate three rollers inside the mouse (an X roller, a Y roller, and a small pressure roller). Use a clean cloth dampened with ammonia solution to clean all of the rollers completely. Use your can of compressed air to blow out any remaining dust or debris that may still be inside the mouse. Finally, replace the mouse ball and secure it into place with its retaining ring.

External Check

Now that the system is clean, it's time to perform a few practical checks of the system interconnections and take care of some basic drive maintenance. Gather a small regular screwdriver (i.e., a jeweler's screwdriver), along with a commercial floppy drive cleaning kit. If your system uses a tape drive, arrange to have a tape drive cleaning kit on hand also. If you cannot locate the appropriate cleaning kits, you can use isopropyl alcohol and long electronics-grade swabs. A hand-held degaussing coil is recommended but may not be necessary. For this part of the maintenance, you'll need to power up the PC.

These checks should be performed every 4 months (three times per year) or as required. If the PC is operating in dusty, industrial, or other adverse environments, you many need to check the system more frequently. Systems operating in clean office environments may only need to be checked once or twice each year.

Step 9: Check cables

There are many external cables interconnecting the computer to its peripheral devices. You should examine each cable and verify that it is securely connected. If the cable can be secured to its connector with screws, make sure that the cable is secured properly. As a minimum, check for the following cables:

- AC power cable for the PC
- AC power cable for the monitor
- AC power cable for the printer
- AC/DC power pack for an external modem (if used)
- Keyboard cable
- Mouse cable
- Joystick cable (if used)
- Video cable to the monitor
- Speaker cable(s) from the sound board
- Microphone cable to the sound board (if used)
- Serial port cable to external modem (if used)
- Parallel port cable to printer
- RJ11 telephone line cable to internal or external modem (if used)

Step 10: Clean the floppy drive

In spite of their age, floppy disks remain a reliable and highly standardized media, and every new PC sold today still carries a 3.5-in 1.44 Mbyte floppy drive. However, floppy disks are a "contact" media—the read/write heads of the floppy drive actually come into contact with the floppy disk. This contact transfers some of the magnetic oxides from the floppy disk to the drive's read/write heads. Eventually, enough oxides can accumulate on the read/write heads to cause reading or writing problems with the floppy drive. You should periodically clean the floppy drive to remove any excess oxides.

Cleaning can be accomplished in several ways. You can use a prepackaged cleaning kit or swab the read/write heads with fresh isopropyl alcohol. You can obtain prepackaged cleaning kits from almost any store that has a computer or consumer electronics department. With a cleaning kit, you simply dampen a mildly abrasive cleaning disk with cleaning solution (typically alcohol-based) and then run the cleaning disk in the drive for 15 to 30 s. You can often get 10 to 20 cleanings from a cleaning disk before discarding it.

If you don't have a cleaning kit handy, you can use a thin fabric swab dampened in fresh isopropyl alcohol and gently scrub between the read/write heads. Remember to turn off and unplug the PC before attempting a manual cleaning. Repeat the scrubbing with several fresh swabs and then use a dry swab to gently dry the heads. Allow several minutes for any residual alcohol to dry before turning the PC back on.

Step 11: Clean the tape drive

As with floppy drives, tape drives are also a contact media, and the tape head is in constant contact with the moving tape. This causes oxides from the tape to transfer to the tape head and capstans, which can ultimately result in reading or writing errors from the tape drive. If a tape drive is present with your system, you should periodically clean the tape head(s) and capstans to remove any dust and excess oxides. You may be able to find a prepackaged drive cleaning kit for your particular tape drive. Otherwise, you'll need to clean the tape drive manually.

Turn off and unplug the PC. Use a thin fabric swab dampened in fresh isopropyl alcohol to gently scrub the tape head(s) and capstan. Repeat the scrubbing with several fresh swabs and then use a dry swab to gently dry the tape head(s). Allow several minutes for any residual alcohol to dry before turning the computer back on.

> **NOTE:** This step is *only* needed if you have an internal or external tape drive with your system. If not, you can omit this step.

Step 12: Check the CD tray

Most CD-ROM drives operate using a tray to hold the CD. Try ejecting and closing the tray several times. Make sure that the motion is smooth and that there is no hesitation or grinding that might suggest a problem with the drive mechanism. While the tray is open, check for any accumulations of dust, pet hair, or other debris in the tray that might interfere with a CD. Clean the tray with a cloth lightly dampened in water *only*. Be sure the tray is completely dry before closing it again. Do not use ammonia or ammonia-based cleaners around the CD-ROM. Prolonged exposure to ammonia vapors can *damage* a CD.

Step 13: Check the sound system

Next, you should make sure that your sound system is set properly. Begin playing an ordinary audio CD in the CD-ROM drive. Check the sound board itself and locate the master volume control (not all sound boards have a physical volume knob). Make sure that the master volume is set at 75 percent or higher. If not, you may need to keep the speaker volume abnormally high, and this can result in a hum or other noise in the speakers. If the sound board does not have a master volume control, check the board's mixer applet to see that the master volume is set properly. Once the sound board is set, you can adjust the speaker volume to achieve the best sound quality.

> **NOTE:** Speakers are magnetic devices that can interfere with the color purity of a monitor. Keep unshielded speakers at least 6 in away from your monitor.

Step 14: Check color purity

Color monitors use a fine metal screen located just behind the CRT face in order to isolate the individual color pixels in the display. This ensures that stray electrons don't strike adjacent phosphors and cause incorrect colors. If part or all of this metal screen becomes magnetized, it will deflect the electron beams and cause color distortion. Normally, a color CRT is demagnetized (or degaussed) each time the monitor is turned on. This is accomplished through a degaussing coil located around the perimeter of the CRT face. However, if the CRT is subjected to external magnetic fields (such as unshielded speakers, motors, or other strong magnets), it may cause color problems across the entire CRT or in small localized areas.

Check the CRT for color purity by displaying an image of a known color (preferably white). Examine the image for discoloration or discolored areas. For example, if you display an image that you know is white, and it appears bluish (or there are bluish patches), chances are that you've got color purity problems.

There are three means of correcting color purity problems. First, try moving anything that might be magnetic (such as speakers) *away* from the monitor. Second, try degaussing the monitor by turning it off, waiting 30 s, and then turning it on again. This allows the monitor's built-in degaussing coil to cycle. If the problem persists, wait 20 to 30 min and try cycling the monitor again. Finally, if the image is still discolored, you should take the monitor to a technician, who can use a hand-held degaussing coil.

Internal Check

At this point, we can move into the PC and perform some internal checks to verify that critical parts and cables are secure and that all cooling systems are working. Internal checks can usually be performed every 6 months (twice per year). Gather a small Philips screwdriver and an antistatic wrist strap. Use your screwdriver to unbolt the outer cover. Remove the outer cover (be careful of sharp edges) and set it aside. Attach the wrist strap from your wrist to a good earth ground. This allows you to work safely inside the PC without the risk of accidental damage from Electrostatic Discharge (ESD).

Step 15: Check the fans

PCs tend to generate a substantial amount of heat during normal operation, and this heat must be ventilated with fans. If one or more fans fail, excess heat can build up in the PC enclosure and result in system crashes or premature system failures. Now that the cover is off, your first check should be to see that all the fans are running. As a minimum, check the power supply fan, the case exhaust fan (both usually located at the rear of the enclosure), and the CPU heat sink/fan. Other PCs such as tower systems may have even more fans. If any fans are not running, they should be replaced, or the system should be serviced by an experienced technician, who can replace defective fans.

Pay particular attention to the CPU heat sink/fan. Virtually all Intel Pentium/Pentium MMX, AMD K5/K6, and Cyrix 6x86/M2 CPUs are fitted with a heat sink/fan. This fan *must* be running, or the CPU runs a very real risk of overheating and failing. If you notice that the fan has stopped, you should have the heat sink/fan assembly replaced *as soon as possible*.

Step 16: Clean fans and filters

Turn off and unplug the PC and then examine the fans and exhaust filters for accumulations of dust or other debris. Use your static-safe vacuum to clean the fan blades. Clean away any accumulations from the exhaust area and then clean the exhaust filter if possible. You may need to remove the exhaust filter for better access. If the exhaust filter is washable, you may choose to rinse the filter in simple soap and water for best cleaning (remember to dry the filter thoroughly before replacing it). Of course, if there is no exhaust filter, simply clean around the exhaust area. Also vacuum away any other accumulations of dust that you may find on the motherboard or around the drives, but be very careful to avoid vacuuming up the little jumpers on the motherboard.

> **NOTE:** Remember that PC electronics are *extremely* sensitive to ESD, so make sure to use a static-safe vacuum inside the PC.

Step 17: Check expansion boards

Most PCs use several expansion boards, which are plugged into expansion slots on the motherboard. Internal modems, video boards, SCSI adapters, and network cards are just a few types of expansion boards that you may encounter. Each expansion board must be inserted completely into its corresponding slot, and the metal mounting bracket on the board should be secured to the chassis with a single screw. Make sure that every board is installed evenly and completely, and see that the mounting bolts are snugged down.

Step 18: Check internal cables

You'll notice that there are a large number of cables inside the PC. Each cable must be installed securely— especially the wide ribbon cable connectors that can easily be tugged off. Take a moment to check any wiring between the case and the motherboard, such as the keyboard connector, power LED, on/off switch, drive activity LED, turbo switch, turbo LED, and so on. Next, check the following cables:

- Motherboard power connector(s)
- All four-pin drive power cables
- Floppy drive ribbon cable
- Hard drive ribbon cable
- CD-ROM ribbon cable (usually separate from the hard drive cable)
- CD four-wire audio cable (between the CD-ROM and sound board)
- SCSI ribbon cable (if used)
- SCSI terminating resistors (if used)

Step 19: Check memory

Memory is provided in the form of SIMMs, which simply clip into sockets on the motherboard. Loose SIMMs can cause serious start-up problems for the

PC. Examine each SIMM to verify that it is inserted properly into its socket and that both ends of each SIMM are clipped into place.

Step 20: Check the CPU

The CPU is the single largest IC on the motherboard and is installed into a ZIF socket for easy replacement or upgrade. Examine the CPU to see that it is inserted evenly into its socket. The ZIF socket lever should be in the closed position and locked down at the socket itself. Check the CPU's heat sink/fan next. It should sit flush against the top of the CPU. It should not slide around or be loose. If it is, the heat sink/fan should be secured or replaced.

Step 21: Check drive mounting

The final step in your internal check should be to inspect the drive mountings. Each drive should be mounted in place with four screws; fewer screws may allow excessive vibration in the drive, which can lead to premature failure. Make sure that each drive has four mounting bolts, and use your Philips screwdriver to snug down each bolt.

> **NOTE:** Do not overtighten the bolts. This can actually warp the drive frame and cause errors or drive failure.

Drive Check

After the PC has been cleaned and checked inside and out, it's time to check the hard drive for potential problems. This involves checking the drive's file system, reorganizing files, and creating an updated boot disk. To perform a drive check, you'll need a copy of ScanDisk and Defrag. These utilities are already built into Windows 95; therefore, you can reboot the system and use those utilities directly. If you are more comfortable with running these utilities from DOS, create a start-up disk and boot from that and then run ScanDisk and Defrag right from the start-up disk. As a rule, you should perform the drive check very regularly—once a month is usually recommended or whenever you make major additions or deletions from your system.

Step 22: Update the boot disk

Your PC should always have a boot disk that can start the system from a floppy drive in the event of an emergency. Windows 95 has the ability to create a start-up disk automatically. If you have access to a Windows 95 system, use the following procedure to create a DOS 7.x start-up disk:

- Label a blank disk and insert it into your floppy drive.
- Click on *Start, Settings,* and *Control Panel.*
- Double-click on the *Add / Remove Programs* icon.
- Select the *Start-up Disk* tab.
- Click on *Create Disk.*
- The utility will remind you to insert a disk and then will prepare the disk automatically. When the preparation is complete, test the disk.

The preparation process takes several minutes and will copy the following files to your disk: ATTRIB, CHKDSK, COMMAND, DEBUG, DRVSPACE.BIN, EDIT, FDISK, FORMAT, REGEDIT, SCANDISK, SYS, and UNINSTAL. All of these files are DOS 7.x-based files, so you can run them from the A: prompt.

Step 23: Run ScanDisk

The ScanDisk utility is designed to check your drive for file problems (such as lost or cross-linked clusters) and then correct those problems. If you're running from the start-up disk, start ScanDisk by typing

```
A:\> SCANDISK <ENTER>
```

If you're running from Windows 95, click *Start, Programs, Accessories, System Tools,* and *ScanDisk.* Select the drive to be tested and start the test cycle. ScanDisk will report any problems and give you the option of repairing them.

Step 24: Run Defrag

Operating systems like DOS and Windows 95 segregate drive space into groups of sectors called *clusters.* Clusters are used on an as found basis, so it is possible for the clusters that compose a file to be scattered across a drive. This forces the drive to work harder (and take longer) to read or write the complete file because a lot of time is wasted moving around the drive. The Defrag utility allows file clusters to be relocated together. If you're running from the start-up disk, start Defrag by typing

```
A:\> DEFRAG <ENTER>
```

If you're running from Windows 95, click *Start, Programs, Accessories, System Tools,* and *Disk Defragmenter.* Select the drive to be tested, and start the cycle. Defrag will relocate every file on the disk so that all their clusters are together.

> **NOTE:** You can run Defrag any time, but you do not *need* to run Defrag until your disk is more than 10 percent fragmented.

Wrap Up

That concludes the maintenance procedure for your PC. Now you can replace the outer cover and bolt it back into place (be careful of sharp edges). After the enclosure is secure, reboot the system and perform a final test of some of the major applications. The system should perform exactly the same as it did before. By performing this routine maintenance, you can keep your PC running longer and save on expensive downtime or trips to the shop.

List of PC Acronyms

AGP	Accelerated Graphics Port
AI	Artificial Intelligence
ALU	Arithmetic Logic Unit (related to CPUs)
AM	Amplitude Modulation (related to modems)
AMD	Advanced Micro Devices, Inc.
AMI	American Megatrends, Inc.
ANSI	American National Standards Institute
ASCII	American Standard Code for Information Interchange
APM	Advanced Power Management
ASIC	Application Specific Integrated Circuit
ASPI	Advanced SCSI Programming Interface
AT	Advanced Technology
ATA	AT bus Attachment
ATAPI	AT Attachment Packet Inference
ATDM	Asynchronous Time Division Multiplexing (related to PC communication)
ATM	Asynchronous Transfer Mode (related to PC communication)

BBS	Bulletin Board System
BCC	Block Check Character
BCD	Binary Coded Decimal
BDA	BIOS Data Area
BE	Back End
BEDO	Burst Extended Data Output
BiCMOS	Bipolar Complementary Metal-Oxide Semiconductor
BIOS	Basic Input/Output System
BNC	Bayonet Nut Connector
BSC	Binary Synchronous Communications (or Bi-Sync)
CAD	Computer Aided Design
CAM	Computer Aided Manufacturing or Common Access Method (Committee)
CAS	Column Address Strobe (related to dynamic memory)
CCD	Charge Coupled Device (related to cameras and video capture)
CCITT	Consultative Committee of International Telephony and Telegraphy
CD	Carrier Detect or Compact Disc
CD-R	Recordable Compact Disc
CDDI	Copper Distributed Data Interface
CD-ROM	Compact Disk Read-Only Memory
CGA	Color Graphics Adapter
CHS	Cylinder Head Sector
CISC	Complex Instruction-Set Computer
CMOS	Complementary Metal-Oxide Semiconductor
COAST	Cache On A Stick
COM	Communication [Port]
CP/M	Control Program/Monitor
CPI	Clocks Per Instruction
CQFP	Ceramic Quad-Flat Pack (related to IC packaging)

CPU	Central Processing Unit
CR	Carriage Return (related to printers)
CRC	Cyclical Redundancy Check
CRQ	Command Response Queue
CRT	Cathode Ray Tube
CS	Chip Select or Cable Select
CSMA	Carrier Sense Multiple-Access (related to PC communication)
CSMA/CD	Carrier Sense Multiple-Access with Collision Detect
CSR	Command Status Register
CTS	Clear To Send
DAT	Digital Audio Tape
DC	Direct Current
DCD	Data Carrier Detect
DCE	Data Circuit-terminating Equipment (related to PC communication)
DD	Double Density
DEC	Digital Equipment Corporation
DES	Data Encryption Standard
DID	Direct Inward Dial
DIMM	Dual Inline Memory Module
DIN	Deutsche Industrie Norm
DIP	Dual Inline Package (related to IC packaging)
DIS	Draft International Standard
DMA	Direct Memory Access
DOS	Disk Operating System
DPE	Data Parity Error
DPSK	Differential Phase Shift Keying (related to PC communication)
DRAM	Dynamic Random Access Memory
DS	Double Sided
DSP	Digital Signal Processor
DSR	Data Set Ready
DTC	Data Terminal Controller

DTE	Data Terminating Equipment (related to PC communication)
DTMF	Dual-Tone Multi-Frequency
DTR	Data Terminal Ready
DVD	Digital Versatile Disc; previously, Digital Video Disc
EBCDIC	Extended Binary Coded Decimal Interchange Code
ECC	Error Correction Code
ECL	Emitter-Coupled Logic
ECO	Engineering Change Order
ECP	Extended Capabilities Port
ECU	EISA Configuration Utility
EDO	Extended Data Output
EEPROM	Electrically Erasable Programmable Read-Only Memory
EGA	Enhanced Graphics Adapter
EIA	Electronic Industries Association
EISA	Enhanced Industry Standard Architecture
EMI	Electro-Magnetic Interference
EMS	Expanded Memory Specification
EOF	End Of File
EOL	End Of Line
EOS	Electrical Over-stress
EPP	Enhanced Parallel Port
EPROM	Erasable Programmable Read-Only Memory
ES	ElectroStatic
ESD	ElectroStatic Discharge
ESDI	Enhanced Small Devices Interface
FAT	File Allocation Table
FCC	Federal Communications Commission
FDC	Floppy Drive Controller
FDD	Fixed Disk Drive or Floppy Disk Drive
FDDI	Fiber Distributed Data Interface
FDM	Frequency Division Multiplexing

FDX	Full-Duplex Transmission
FE	Front End
FEP	Front End Processor
FF	Form Feed (related to printers)
FIFO	First-In First-Out
FILO	First-In Last-Out (same as LIFO)
FM	Frequency Modulation (related to modems)
FPGA	Field Programmable Gate Array (related to IC packaging)
FPM	Fast Page Mode
FPU	Floating Point Unit (related to microprocessors)
FRU	Field-Replaceable Unit
FSF	Free Software Foundation
FSK	Frequency Shifty Keying (related to modems)
FTP	File Transfer Program
GAS	Gallium Arsenide
GNU	Gnu's Not Unix
GUI	Graphical User Interface
HD	High Density
HDC	Hard Drive Controller
HDD	Hard Disk Drive
HDX	Half-Duplex Transmission
HFS	Hierarchical File System
HPFS	High Performance File System
HS	Helical Scan
I/O	Input/Output
IBM	International Business Machines Corp.
IC	Integrated Circuit
ICU	ISA Configuration Utility
ID	Identification
IDC	Insulation Displacement Connector
IDE	Integrated Device Electronics or Integrated Drive Electronics

IEEE	Institute of Electrical and Electronic Engineers
IMP	Interface Message Processor
IPC	Inter-Process Communication
IPL	Initial Program Load
IRQ	Interrupt Request
ISA	Industry Standard Architecture
ISDN	Integrated Services Digital Network
ISO	International Standards Organization
ISP	Internet Service Providers
ISDN	Integrated Services Digital Network
JFS	Journaled File System
LAN	Local Area Network
LAPM	Link Access Procedure M
LBA	Logical Block Addressing
LCD	Liquid Crystal Display
LED	Light Emitting Diode
LF	Line Feed (related to printers)
LFB	Linear Frame Buffer
LIM	Lotus/Intel/Microsoft Expanded Memory Manager Specification
LPT	Line Printer Terminal (or simply "Printer Port")
LRU	Least-Recently Used
LSB/lsb	Least Significant Byte/bit
LSI	Large Scale Integration
LUN	Logical Unit Number (related to SCSI)
MAN	Metropolitan Area Network
MBR	Master Boot Record
MCA	Micro Channel Architecture
MCGA	Multi-Color Graphics Array
MCM	Multi-Chip Module (related to IC packaging)
MFLOPS	Millions (10^6) of Floating Point Operations per Second (or MegaFlops)
MFM	Modified Frequency Modulated

MICR	Magnetic Ink Character Recognition
MIDI	Musical Instrument Digital Interface
MIMD	Multiple-Instruction Multiple-Data
MIPS	Millions of Instructions per Second
MISD	Multiple-Instruction Single Data
MMU	Memory Management Unit
MMX	Multimedia Extension (related to advanced microprocessors)
MNP	Microcom Network Protocol (related to PC communication)
MODEM	Modulator/Demodulator
MOPS	Millions of Operations Per Second
MOS	Metal-Oxide Semiconductor
MP	Multi-Processor
MPEG	Motion Picture Experts Group
MPP	Massively Parallel Processor
MSB/msb	Most Significant Byte/bit
MS-DOS	Microsoft Disk Operating System
MSI	Medium Scale Integration
MTBF	Mean Time Between Failure
N/C	No Connection or No Contact
NBS	National Bureau of Standards
NEMA	National Electrical Manufacturers Association
NFS	Network File System
NFU	Not-Frequently Used
NMI	Non-Maskable Interrupt
NMOS	Negatively doped Metal-Oxide Semiconductor
NOP	No Operation
NRU	Not-Recently Used
NSF	National Science Foundation
NVRAM	Non-Volatile Random Access Memory
OCR	Optical Character Recognition (related to scanners)
ODI	Open Datalink Interface

OEM	Original Equipment Manufacturer
OS	Operating System
OSF	Open Software Foundation
OSI	Open Systems Interconnect
PAL/PLA	Programmable Array Logic (Logic Array)
PB	Push Button
PC	Personal Computer or Program Counter
PCB	Printed Circuit Board
PCI	Peripheral Component Interconnect
PCM	Pulse Code Modulation
PCMCIA	Personal Computer Memory Card International Association
PE	Processor Element
PFF	Page Fault Frequency
PGA	Pin Grid Array (related to IC packaging)
PIC	Programmable Interrupt Controller
PIO	Programmed Input/Output
PLCC	Plastic Leaded Chip Carrier (related to IC packaging)
PLL	Phase Locked Loop
PM	Preventive Maintenance
PMOS	Positively doped Metal-Oxide Semiconductor
PnP	Plug-and-Play
POST	Power-On Self-Test
POTS	Plain Old Telephone Service
PPP	Point-to-Point Protocol
PQFP	Plastic Quad-Flat Pack (related to IC packaging)
PROM	Programmable Read-Only Memory
PSTN	Public Switched Telephone Network
PTE	Page Table Entry
QAM	Quadrature Amplitude Modulation (related to modems)

QFP	Quad-Flat Pack (related to IC packaging)
QIC	Quarter Inch Cartridge (Committee)
RAID	Redundant Arrays of Inexpensive Disks
RAM	Random Access Memory
RAMDAC	Random Access Memory Digital-to-Analog Converter
RAS	Row Address Strobe (related to dynamic memory)
RCA	Radio Corporation of America
RCC	Routing Control Center
RFC	Request For Comments
RFI	Radio Frequency Interference
RI	Ring Indicator
RISC	Reduced Instruction-Set Computer
RLL	Run Length Limited
RMM	Read Mostly Memory (same as EPROM)
rms	root mean squared
RMW	Read Modify Write
ROM	Read-Only Memory
RPC	Remote Procedure Call
RPM	Rotations Per Minute
RTC	Real Time Clock
RTS	Request To Send
R/W	Read/Write
SAM	Sequential Access Memory
SASI	Shugart Associates Standard Interface
SCSI	Small Computer Systems Interface
SD	Single Density
SDLC	Synchronous Data Link Control
SDRAM	Synchronous Dynamic Random Access Memory
SEC	Single Edge Contact
SIMD	Single-Instruction Multiple-Data
SIMM	Single Inline Memory Module

SIPP	Single Inline Pinned Package (related to IC packaging)
SISD	Single-Instruction Single-Data
SLIP	Serial Line Internet Protocol
SMD	Surface Mount Device
SMP	Symmetric Multiprocessing
SMT	Surface Mount Technology
SNA	System Network Architecture
SNR	Signal-to-Noise Ratio
SO/SOL	Small Outline
SOIC	Small Outline Integrated Circuit
SPOOL	Simultaneous Peripheral Operation On Line
SPT	Sectors Per Track
SPU	Single Processor Unit
SQE	Signal Quality Error
SRAM	Static Random Access Memory
SS	Single Sided
SVTP	Standard Voltage and Timing Parameter
STDM	Synchronous Time Division Multiplexing
STN	Super Twisted Nematic
STU	Streaming Tape Unit
SVGA	Super Video Graphics Array
TCM	Trellis Code Modulation (related to modems)
TCP/IP	Transmission Control Protocol/Internet Protocol
TDM	Time Division Multiplexing
TI	Texas Instruments
TIA	Telecommunications Industry Association
TPI	Tracks Per Inch
TSR	Terminate and Stay Resident
TTL	Transistor-Transistor Logic
TUV	Technischer Ueberwachuags Verein
UART	Universal Asynchronous Receiver/Transmitter
UDP	User Datagram Protocol

UMA	Upper Memory Area
UMB	Upper Memory Block
UPS	Uninterruptible Power Supply
USB	Universal Serial Bus
USL	Unix System Labs
UTP	Unshielded Twisted Pair
UUCP	Unix to Unix Copy Program
VCR	Video Cassette Recorder
VESA	Video Electronics Standards Association
VGA	Video Graphics Array
VLB	VESA Local Bus or Video Local Bus
VLIW	Very Long Instruction Word
VLSI	Very Large Scale Integration
VM	Virtual Memory
VME	Versa Module Eurocard
VRAM	Video Random Access Memory
VRM	Reduced Voltage Mode
VRM	Voltage Regulator Module
VTR	Video Tape Recorder
VXD	Virtual Driver
WAN	Wide Area Network
WATS	Wide Area Telephone Service
WD	Western Digital
WORM	Write-Once Read-Many
WS	Wait State
XGA	Extended Graphics Array
XMS	Extended Memory Specification
XOR	Exclusive-Or
XT	Extended Technology
ZIF	Zero Insertion Force

ABOUT THE AUTHOR

Stephen Bigelow is an experienced computer professional, teacher, and founder of Dynamic Learning Systems. He has written more than 90 feature articles and several books on computer hardware and electronics, including *Bigelow's PC Technicians Troubleshooting Pocket Reference, Bigelow's Computer Repair Toolkit*, and the highly popular *Troubleshooting and Repairing* titles from McGraw-Hill. He conducts the online "Build Your Own PC" course for Ziff Davis University (www.zdu.com), which attracts hundreds of students each semester. He also co-hosts "PC TechLine," a weekly call-in radio show. This interaction with end users lends a truly practical slant to his work. Stephen Bigelow is a graduate of Central New England College and lives in Jefferson, Massachusetts.

Index